falconry

falconry

HUMPHREY ap EVANS

John Bartholomew
Edinburgh

Endpapers: drawings of a hawk from the nest
through to full maturity are by Otto Kals, the famous
hawk equipment maker and artist from Düsseldorf,
Germany, who died in the summer of 1972.
His widow presented many of his drawings and
paintings to the author of this book.

© Humphrey ap Evans 1973
First published 1973
by John Bartholomew and Son Ltd.
12 Duncan Street, Edinburgh EH9 1TA
Also at 216 High Street, Bromley BR1 1PW
ISBN 0 85152 921 6

Designed and edited by Youé and Spooner Ltd.

Printed in Great Britain

ACKNOWLEDGMENTS

I am very grateful to the many falconers and hawking enthusiasts who have so generously helped me, in one way or another, in connection with this introduction to the world of hawking, and in particular to those who have so kindly allowed me to use many of their own photographs to illustrate various points throughout the book. My special thanks are due to Mr. John Morris, who is not only a highly skilled falconer himself, but is one of Ireland's leading photographers; to lend the copyright of many of his fine pictures puts me particularly in his debt.

I should also like to thank the many enthusiasts in Britain and other parts of the world who get in touch with me to ask: 'What shall I do next?' and 'What do you think went wrong?' I am constantly learning new things, almost as much from the unknown beginner who seriously wishes to make a start, as from the experienced falconers, among whom I am proud to count so many as friends or acquaintances.

I should like to say thank you also to the small number of patrons in the grand traditional manner who are maintaining or building establishments today well worthy of any of those of the great days of the past, about which we read endlessly in the classic handbooks. They are doing the greatest possible service to the cause of falconry throughout the world. If this book becomes the first step for even one beginner to make his way eventually into their company, then it will have been well worthwhile.

Among the people who have allowed me to use their photographs or have helped me in other ways with illustrations are:

Lorant de Bastyai
Beaverbrook Newspapers
Hans Brehm
Jim Brown
J. M. Buckner
Sqn. Ldr. N. C. Cargill, RAF
Kent Carnie
Cecil Clifton
Mike Clowes
H. C. R. P. Combe

A. C. Cowper Ltd.
Walter Crammer
David S. Gosmore
James Gow
Col. R. A. Graham
Robin Haigh
Frances Hamerstrom
Frau Otto Kals
The Keighley News
Sir Khizar Hayat Khan, Tiwana
John Loft
Colonel William Mattox
J. McFarlane
Farquhar McKechnie
Dr. Ridley McPhail
Mike Melvill
Dr. Heinz Meng
François Merlet
C. V. Middleton & Son
Sydney Moore
The Honourable Johnny Morris
George Mussared
Paris-Match
Geoffrey Pollard
Paul Popper Agency
Croft Slater
Christopher Snelling
Ronald Stevens
Count Fulco Tosti
Lord Tweedsmuir
United Newspapers Ltd.
Renz Waller
Welsh Hawking Club
L. Workman

INTRODUCTION

This book is not for the expert. He has already read everything or knows everything, has no need of help or advice from anyone and will sort out his problems in his own way, which will be far best.

This is for the person who is starting an interest in hawks, or thinks he may be doing so. I hope the many discouraging aspects will down the dabbler. Hawks are getting more and more difficult to obtain. Those people who get hold of them illegally or by devious means, only to let them die through ignorance or lack of all possible precautions against illness or accident, do a greater disservice than ever to that magnificent tribe of birds, the hawks and falcons. The birds are under pressure from many sides, and it would be very wrong to add to their hazards by thoughtless or wanton treatment.

This does not mean to say that even the most ardent will not lose his hawk by illness or accident – of course he will. But the point is that he is doing all he can to prevent this, while building up that great and exciting relationship between a human being and a hawk, which has drawn so many to the study and practice of falconry.

But I hope this may be a small encouragement to the beginner to take the subject seriously and to persevere throughout all the difficulties which lie in his way. He or she will find it well worth it, and will never regret any time spent in the company of a hawk, however wild, cross and apparently unco-operative she seems to be.

He will not find here details on how to prepare and fly a cast of peregrines at grouse, nor a programme for a season's partridge hawking in the grand manner. But he will, I hope, find encouragement to start in the right direction and to prepare himself in the greatly changed modern conditions to get the greatest pleasure from what is available today. This can be a good foundation for leading on to the highest flights of game hawking to which all true falconers will aspire but few ever attain. For more detailed study of all the aspects of hawking and falconry which he is likely to encounter and may wish to learn, the reader is recommended to study the companion volume, *Falconry For You*

(Foyle's), which is a complete handbook.

By the time he reaches a peak of skill and opportunity he will have learnt all he wants to know and will need only the experience. There are many publications on the subject with varying degrees of learning and usefulness, some deeply specialized and particularly valuable for the distillation of years of experience to be found in them. It is very much to be hoped that the falconer will wish to add to his shelves everything written on the subject which his purse will allow.

The purpose of this book is to encourage him to set foot on the accepted way and to join with others in this interest to strengthen the hand of those who are working to keep hawking alive and flourishing.

The secret of immortality has not been disclosed to falconers any more than to other groups of human beings. The present generation of practising falconers, whose skill in many cases will be the equal to that of any of the great names of the past, will not, alas, be able to run after their hawks for ever.

It is for this reason that, throughout the 25 years of my membership of the British Falconers' Club, I have always sought to encourage new people to seek out the friendship or acquaintance of as many of the present-day falconers as they can, and to absorb some of the expertise from them – the sort which can never be learnt from books.

Without new people the sport will soon die. There are many who would welcome its relegation to exhibits in county museums. There is an understandable tendency to try to restrict new interest to the utmost degree. There are not enough hawks to go round and in some cases they are getting fewer. Some sections of the community, concerned about the survival of birds in general, would like to see all forms of falconry banned, a possibility already being discussed in government quarters.

But who could be more intensely interested in the survival of hawks than falconers themselves?

Now is the time for more interest, more study, more practical work in all departments of falconry, so that the ancient skills, so hardly learnt and difficult to practise, shall not be phased out in Britain for all time.

CHAPTER 1

What is the state of hawking and falconry in the modern world? How is it being affected by the rapidly increasing pressures on wild life, and on birds in particular? How are people themselves treating this most exacting of all relationships between humans and non-humans?

It is generally understood that people today have less and less time to spend on activities which require gentle patience and give unspectacular results. Under these conditions, with the world apparently in a state of galloping frenzy, there is much encouragement to be had from the fact that hawking has never been so popular in Britain and in several parts of Europe since the 18th century, or even earlier. In North America, it has a very highly skilled and growing following.

Unfortunately, this resurgence of interest has coincided with one or two very serious problems. Chief among these has been the vastly widespread and largely indiscriminate use of lethal chemicals in all aspects of land use. Birds are probably the chief sufferers from this unending attack, and birds of prey in particular. A hawk in pursuit of her quarry will naturally take the one which looks as if it will need the least effort to capture. If the quarry is flying more slowly than others because of some creeping poisoning from its natural food the hawk, of course, takes it and guarantees herself one more dose of chemicals which she may or may not be able to counteract by her natural digestion. If it is true that over 50 per cent of all wild birds are probably living and flying at less than 75 per cent efficiency due to their absorption of potentially lethal chemicals, it does not take long to understand why the native populations of hawks in many countries, and in Britain in particular, are on the decrease.

But chemicals are not the only reason why birds of prey which can be used for hawking are in decline. The growth of interest in shooting in Britain has been spectacular. Thousands of shotguns are sold every year to people now discovering the delights of wandering about the countryside firing with impunity at anything which turns up. New regulations, designed to curb this over-rapid growth, have done very little to

Although this male buzzard is undoubtedly beautiful to look at and a nice hawk for a beginner to train, he is slack mettled.

This drawing, after Landseer's original, depicts a nineteenth-century falconer with his cadge of peregrines and a couple of spaniel-type dogs.

protect the wild birds and animals from such widespread assault. People are encouraged on all sides by more new gun clubs and wildfowling associations to join up, get a gun and start firing. Membership of almost any gun club paves the way to the granting of shotgun licence.

In addition to these pressures, organised shooting of game on traditional lines has become so valuable that the attitude of keepers and owners of shoots which, over the past decade, had shown signs of increasing sympathy towards the native hawks, has recently hardened perceptibly. This particular problem is easy to see. The rent of a grouse moor today will be in the region of £4 to £5 a brace shot. Anyone wanting to buy a grouse moor will have to pay on a basis of £150 to £200 a brace of grouse, reckoned on the numbers of grouse shot during the previous few seasons. If the first consideration is the fee that can be obtained for a let or a sale, the odd peregrine cleaving the highland air with that incomparable dark glitter and swish of wind will be fortunate if she does not find the contents of a full choke accompanying her into the clouds.

Kestrels abound in many districts throughout Britain but they appear to be more and more localized. This may be due to the comparative reactions of their prey to the type of chemical treatment which the land has been receiving in that particular district. They remain the best bird for anyone wanting to learn about hawking and they are the most readily available. A licence to acquire one would not reasonably be withheld from anyone wanting to make a start.

Sparrowhawks have vanished altogether from many districts. The next 10 years may be crucial for them, showing whether they are set on the slope to extinction like the beautiful and little known hobby, now under 100 pairs strong in Britain, or whether they can hold on and recover.

The other great favourite of the falconer, the merlin, seems to be excessively scarce, and sadly may also be on the way out.

Ironically, this picture of gloom is set in a frame of the greatly increased interest in training hawks now to be seen on all sides in Britain and also abroad. No game or country fair is now complete without its colourful collection of hawks of all sorts sitting out on blocks in dog-proof weathering grounds, and probably a display of some hawks exercising to the lure before a hushed audience of many hundreds. These displays are always memorable and excite great interest in hawks and everything to do with birds of prey. Hawking Club tents are besieged by people wanting to take up hawking. Bird dealers report a lively upsurge of interest in their advertisements in newspapers and magazines in which birds are regularly offered for sale during the weeks immediately following one of these displays. The average result is an ill-managed hawk mouldering away in a draughty pen while its owner bewails its lack of co-operation.

But every now and again the interest of one person is aroused which leads him on to study the whole business of training a hawk. He learns everything he can about the job, he gets in touch with a club or with other falconers, and a new hawking man or woman emerges to join the small band of freelance and club members who are taking a daily delight in their association with a hawk which they have trained themselves. Many, of course, fall by the wayside, both hawk and hawker, falcon and falconer. But falconry is not the only sphere of activity where this occurs and is surely more exacting than most.

The chief difficulty found in starting to train a hawk is to get hold of a hawk to train. We have seen that there are fewer native hawks in Britain every year, and that there are more people wanting one every year. It is an awkward situation. The well-established falconer who has served a long apprenticeship over the years has obtained his hawk with difficulty, has trained her and held on to her through accident, disease and threat of theft (a comparatively new and increasing threat) and, above all, who has caught quarry with her, will naturally resent new people coming in to the sport and competing for the decreasing number of hawks available.

It is widely held among some established falconers that everyone in the sport should lie low, say nothing and maybe all the new people will lose interest.

One of the most famous strains of peregrines, used since time immemorial, comes from the Isle of Man. Appropriately called Manxman, this one has claimed a fine score of partridge for his owner, Mr. Sydney Moore. There is still rumoured to be an occasional pair on the island but I have not heard of any eyasses being reported recently.

On the other hand, it is held that the more people who can be made seriously interested in this most exciting of all natural sports, the better chance there is of more hawks surviving in the wild. There is also less chance of arrogant legislators and conservational cranks getting falconry placed on the illegal or suspended list of activities, along with coursing, hunting and other traditional sports.

What is the solution? My belief is that the greater safety for the whole world of hawks and hawking lies in a wider knowledge and understanding of the matter. The less people know about hawking, the more vulnerable the activity becomes. I would not have held this opinion some decades ago, since there was a time not far distant when people could pursue their own enjoyments without undue interference.

There was a wider attitude of live and let live, and more tolerance in general life. But today, the urge to condemn, knowing little or nothing about the subject and being unwilling to learn about it, is very pervasive.

Hooligans run screaming among meets of hounds scattering marbles and broken glass round horses and hounds and squirting canisters of strong-smelling fluids to prevent a line being followed. Men lie in bushes with long focus lenses at coursing meetings, hoping to photograph scenes of sufficiently outrageous cruelty to support the wild claims printed in anti-coursing propaganda. Police are sent by anonymous informers to the houses of falconers with claims that their bird has killed something, that it is wicked and should be banned.

I recommend a visit to the local slaughterhouse to

anyone whom ignorance or suppressed hypocrisy compel to raise a clamour against such age-old skills. Nature's way in life and death is cruel indeed, but undisguised. As far as falconry is concerned, the sport needs as many well informed, tolerant and articulate supporters as it can get. The aim of all falconers is the continuance of his sport, pastime, skill or hobby, however he wishes to describe it. Any who genuinely wish to join their ranks should be made welcome in the interests of survival of the sport, and this attitude is now widely prevalent.

But the difficulties today are greater than ever and the discouragements far more formidable. Without a licence from the Home Office, in England and Wales, or the Scottish Department, in Scotland, it is impossible to obtain a native hawk legally in Britain. Special licences are also needed now to import a hawk from abroad, and the resulting expense and general performance involved in this is a serious obstacle to most beginners.

This has had the effect of saving the life of many hawks which were otherwise freely taken from nests in Britain, trapped as adults, or – in the case of foreign hawks – freely imported by dealers and sold to anyone who would pay the price, regardless of whether he had the knowledge or conditions to receive, feed and train the bird. But it has also had the effect of discouraging many a young man with a deep and genuine love of birds from becoming a devoted student of hawks and a practising falconer. It has also greatly encouraged the robbing of nests of their young by the increasing number of people prepared to disregard this law, to the great disadvantage of the law-abiding but frustrated falconer who finds himself unable to replace a lost hawk without vast expense and time spent which he may well not be able to afford.

The nest robbers find a ready market for peregrines in particular, and are not lacking in resourcefulness, courage or money on most occasions. Two years ago on the Pembrokeshire coast, a man swam nearly a mile through the treacherous swell to reach the base of a sheer rock face, swarmed up, removed the eyasses, and swam safely back with them. A year ago, a keeper in Scotland was given £50 to turn a blind eye while a robber stole eyasses from an eyrie which the keeper's employer wished to preserve. Few keepers would be so disloyal and fewer still accept money under such circumstances, but it is wrong that a law, impossible to enforce and misdirected in its application, should bring such a situation into being.

We must ask again, what is the beginner to do, and how is he to do it? Is he to forget the whole thing and take up the breeding of budgerigars as less taxing and certainly more profitable? Or is he to tackle the situation as he finds it today, joining with those who already take immeasurable pleasure in an association with hawks of some sort or another, and look forward to a lifetime of interest in this greatest of all man's associations with the wild?

CHAPTER 2

How is anyone to make a start? Where do you get a
hawk from and what sort of hawk do you try to get?

Only a few years ago this was the least of the problems. If you lived in the country there would be little
difficulty in going round the district asking suitable
people, such as keepers or even local policemen, if they
had seen any kestrels, supposing you did not yourself
know where there was likely to be a pair. As soon as
a good kestrel haunt was discovered, a polite approach
to the owner of the ground for permission to take a
young bird from the nest in the early summer would
usually be well enough received. It only remained to
climb the tree or get someone more nimble and fear-
less if necessary, to remove a young bird carefully,
either from the nest or from the surrounding branches.

But it is now necessary to get a licence to carry out
this operation, either from the Home Office, Protection
of Birds Committee, Westminster, London, SW1,
if the bird is to come from England or Wales, or from
the Scottish Home Department, St. Andrews House,
Edinburgh, if the bird is to be taken in Scotland. This
procedure applies to all birds of prey in Britain.

The native kestrel is undoubtedly the best bird to
start with, since it is not scarce in many districts, will
become tame very quickly if a little concentrated time
is spent on it, and will fly very well in an uncomplain-
ing way and in comparatively cramped conditions. It
can be exercised and flown quite adequately in a town
or a district where there are very few open spaces. It
therefore has the great advantage of not requiring
extensive flying grounds and an elaborate procedure
before going into action.

No pheasant, partridge or rook has to be produced
for it to fly at. It will try for sparrows, starlings, even
mice and similar less exotic quarry. You will have a
lot of fun with one, under the most modest conditions
as well as in more favourable surroundings. It can be
trained to hover on demand, which is very pretty and
satisfying to see.

Licences to obtain one are not normally withheld
unreasonably, provided the applicant can show that
he means to keep the bird in proper conditions and
for his own purposes.

14

Lelia, a peregrine falcon, displays the conformation
of a longwing. Her owner is Mr. Ronald Stevens,
one of Europe's foremost masters of falconry
in all its aspects.

Mr. Ronald Stevens casts off Lelia.

But before going to this length, it is well worth trying to get in touch with someone who has a hawk himself at the moment, or at least who has had one at some time. It is very rare that someone with experience, however slight, will not be ready to tell a serious beginner all they know.

It is well worth reading the one or two modern handbooks which are now available before even doing this, since it saves a lot of unnecessary questioning. Also, it is easier to get a more sympathetic hearing if you can show that you have at least tried to learn up a bit about it, and are not expecting to be told the most elementary details.

The price of the old, standard hawking books, stuffed with generations of experience and tips, some more useful than others, has become ridiculous, due to the unfortunate interest in the subject being taken by mere book collectors. It is not unusual to find some of the early classics being offered – and apparently bought – for up to £100 each and £20 or £30 is commonplace. Thus the beginner, unless particularly well heeled, has no hope of getting hold of one. The public libraries are only partially helpful, since the book needs to be on the shelf at home at all times, ready for immediate reference.

But fortunately new methods of photo copying are being increasingly widely applied to the reprinting of scarce and therefore expensive books. This is bringing some of them within reach of many enthusiasts, but they still remain at several pounds. No beginner should be unduly dismayed at not being able to buy books. One or two of the cheaper ones are quite adequate. There is a note about these in the bibliography at the end of this book.

The best advice is to read the one which seems most clearly laid out. Then to try to get in touch with a practising falconer or someone who goes out with a hawk, whether he feels grand enough to call himself a falconer or not.

Falcon is a word strictly applied only to a female peregrine, generally considered the finest European bird for the purpose, and certainly now the most highly prized and, in Britain, the most difficult to

Opposite: 'A green thought in a green shade' – my peregrine falcon, Corrie.

The drawing by Charles Gere, 1934, is of Lord
Tweedsmuir holding his famous goshawk,
Jezebel, who was one of the great hawk characters
between the wars. Over the years, Jezebel took a
vast number of rabbits and all manner of other
quarry, finally ending her life tragically by taking
stand on an electric pylon. In defiance of all
scientific reason, she exploded in a shower of
sparks, flame and smoke, a fitting end, perhaps, to
one of the most formidable goshawks on record.

acquire. She is a true falcon, having long sickle wings
and dark brown eyes, as well as a notch on either side
of her beak. All the hawks with dark eyes are more like
the peregrine than the other class of hawks, known as
the 'shortwinged' hawks, as opposed to the true
'longwinged' falcons.

The shortwing hawks being less high flying are the
most suitable for close or wooded countryside. The
person owning and flying a peregrine, or any of her
tribe such as the hawks from the Middle Eastern
deserts, can call himself a falconer without fear of
contradiction. The sportsman who habitually works
one of the shortwings with its golden eye, broader
wings and more swooping, ground-level flight, might
hesitate before describing himself as a falconer. His
bird may be a goshawk or sparrowhawk or some
foreign bird, and he may not wish to be called a falconer. But it is a matter of surprisingly little importance to anyone else to whom anyone with any sort
of hawk is a falconer, plain and simple.

The next stage before actually acquiring a bird, or
perhaps simultaneously with putting in hand the business of trying to get hold of a hawk, is to write to the
Secretary of a Hawking Club. The current addresses
of two of these are: The Hon. Secretary, British
Falconers' Club, Yorke House, Hannington, near
Swindon, Wiltshire, and The Hon. Secretary, Welsh
Hawking Club, 63 Wenallt Road, Rhiwbina, Cardiff.
These addresses are liable to change, of course, but
they make the best point of contact with the hawking
world for the beginner.

He must not expect to be welcomed at once with
open arms. In a sphere where it is already so difficult
to find birds to train, newcomers will readily understand that it is only reasonable for them to serve a sort
of probationary period before being admitted as full
members. But the Club Secretary will probably be
ready to tell the applicant of the whereabouts of the
existing member nearest to him. It is then up to the
hopeful learner to persuade the member to give him
a hand, or at least a little practical advice. This would
only rarely not be given willingly enough.

If he shows himself genuinely keen to learn, and has

Three members of the Welsh Hawking Club, Clwb Hebogwyr Cymru, one of the most vigorous of the newer national and international clubs. On the right of the picture is the President, Mr. Lorant de Bastyai holding his lanner. In the centre is the Club Treasurer, Mr. J. M. Buckner with his American red-tailed hawk and on the left is club member Mr. Brian Baynton with a particularly fine-looking adult female goshawk.

not just had a passing fancy worked up by seeing films on falconry, or heard a lecture with coloured slides, the beginner may well come to be accepted as a potentially useful member of the Club or Society, and eventually be admitted to full membership.

The difficulties in all this are not being made light of, since today it is increasingly important that the diminishing resources available to the really keen falconer, or man with a hawk, are not diluted by casual enquirers and people who have no serious intention of taking up the sport in a meaningful way.

Conversely, it is equally important that no one who is becoming genuinely interested should be choked off, since the sport needs all the firm support it can get. The more people who are closely allied to clubs or societies devoted to hawks and their training, management and flying, the less easy it will be for official obstacles to build up to the stage where all forms of hawking or falconry are banned by law.

That such a dire situation is being canvassed in some quarters, and is even already visualized by some res-

ponsible people having the authority to set banning procedure in motion, is illustrated by a recent letter on the subject of granting licences to accredited falconers. It was written by the Chairman of the two Committees, in England and in Scotland, in reply to a query about his policy. It is a matter of great importance and should be widely known so that all who are interested in the continuance of this great sport can be forewarned of what may be in the offing.

The first letter, an extract of which appears further on, questions the wisdom of refusing to give any licence to take a peregrine in Britain, even to the most experienced falconer flying peregrines every season on the moors or on partridge grounds, or rook hawking on the downs. The only exceptions have apparently been to establishments using peregrines to keep runways clear at Service aerodromes about which there will be more in a later chapter.

The reply, also printed later, is from Professor Wynne Edwards, a Fellow of the Royal Society and, at the present time, Chairman of the Home Office

Advisory Committee on the Protection of Birds in England and Wales as well as of the equivalent Home Department Committee. His opinion therefore reflects the official attitude. It is an additionally strong reason for all who are interested in hawks and hawking to join a recognized club; by thus supporting an organized body of opinion there is more chance of falconry not being made so difficult that hardly anyone will be able to carry it on. The disruptive activities of the increasing number of individuals who flout the law by taking birds illegally not only act unfairly to the great majority of falconers who at the moment still respect the law, but they hasten the day when the more important native hawks will have vanished from Britain altogether.

The following is the edited extract from the letter to Professor Wynne Edwards:

'*I would be most grateful if you would help me in my replies to the people who write from time to time in distress at not being granted a licence to take a home bred peregrine eyass for the purposes of falconry.*'

Licences for kestrels and occasionally sparrowhawks, but not merlins, are usually not withheld unless there are special reasons. Buzzards do not really come into this category, since although they are very beautiful to look at, they are slack mettled birds, preferring to play a waiting game for small quarry to come their way, rather than dashing to the attack like the more favoured birds which can be found in a falconer's mews.

'*The increased native population of peregrines in Scotland has, as you will know, coincided with a growing awareness by other countries of the necessity of looking after their own birds more satisfactorily, and also with a possible decline of raptors in Spain, Italy and the Middle East, from which it was possible to obtain longwings for hawking.*

'*The present blanket restriction by your Committees on all licence applications, apart from Service uses, to take peregrines for hawking is having two main effects:*

'*(1) making it increasingly difficult for existing falconers to practise the highest form of the art of falconry by flying peregrines and impossible for newcomers to gain*

the expertise.

'*(2) driving the less scrupulous enthusiasts to break the law in stealing eyasses and trapping adult birds in secrecy, and bribing keepers and others to assist them, or to act on their behalf for large payments. From my own knowledge, I know this to be happening on an increasing scale.*

'*The official answer from your Government office in reply to queries about licences is: get the birds from Canada or Hong Kong or somewhere else. Most falconers cannot afford this, and such a course, even on the rare occasions when it is remotely feasible, is beyond their means. They feel – and many would agree – that with Britain the cradle of modern falconry in Europe, British falconers and aspiring falconers should, however sparingly, be given a chance now and again to practise the ancient art which has endured for so long.*

'*Even a limited number of licences granted would be greatly appreciated and would do much to keep the sport alive: the hawking fraternity would, I am sure, well understand and accept that it was better for a few licences to be granted on a highly selective basis than for none at all, as at present. The slight reduction in the use of widespread agricultural poisons, which has allowed the home stock of peregrines in Britain to begin to recover from the disastrous past two or three decades gives added point to this argument.*'

This granting of a few licences each year would not just be a case of the very few established experts being able to obtain whatever they wanted, with no one else getting a look in. With a regular, though small, supply of home birds coming into falconers' hands every year, it would mean that gradually more birds would filter out to those coming into the sport. A beginner who now wishes to take up hawking has practically no hope at all of coming on to the peregrine after he has served his exacting apprenticeship of kestrel handling, studying, and watching others managing their hawks.

'*As you will be aware, peregrines used for hawking are not infrequently lost, thereby returning to the wild, and also if they reach a ripe age or develop some characteristic making them unsuitable for hawking, may also be returned – or hacked back to the wild, as it is called –*

Herr Brehm shows what an eagle can do.

so wastage in the proper hands is very small in relation to the available supply.

'I would be so grateful for your opinion on the subject, and for any indication you may be able to give me that the present policy is not to endure for the foreseeable future.'

The Professor's reply was a disturbing one for those interested in the legal survival of falconry in Britain.

'We are naturally keen to see the native peregrine population strongly re-established, and our opinion is that it is better not to grant licences to private individuals for the time being. But there would be no objection in principle to allowing a small crop of eyasses to be taken if things went well in the next few years.'

This sounds all right, but in fact it is not working. It is thought by many people that more eyasses or nestlings are being removed, now that it is illegal and not possible to get a licence, than there were when there was either a reasonable granting of licences, or no licences needed at all. The many keen falconers saw to the widespread protection of many nests, and owners and keepers on the spot tended to protect the nests, knowing that one or two would be needed each year for the regular visiting falconer. There was also a much greater collective spirit of protection and fostering of pairs of peregrines than exists today. It rankles with many seasoned falconers that they are not granted even an occasional licence, yet less scrupulous people are taking them without thought of the law, and apparently without any retribution. A large percentage of these stolen birds – which they can only rightly be considered – are sold covertly abroad, mostly to Germany. The Professor's letter concludes:

'The illegal taking and also killing of peregrines is a serious problem. I imagine that if it grew to the point where it jeopardized the survival of the peregrine as a breeding species in any part of the country, Parliament would give priority to saving the peregrine, and so probably would the falconers, even though the only effective remedy might be to suspend or ban falconry altogether.'

It is a most serious affair if it is being thought in official circles that the whole realm of falconry may be made an illegal activity, like cock fighting, simply

because the number of home bred peregrines begins to decline. If the number of sparrowhawks, for instance, declines much further, is the whole of falconry still to lie under such a threat of Parliamentary extinction, stimulated by government Bird Protection Committees?

This must be a disturbing thought, especially when it is realized that a heavy toll of eyasses is being taken every year with apparent impunity.

But questions of obtaining a peregrine and whether they will survive or not, need only affect a beginner indirectly. They should not prevent him devoting time to the several other branches of the sport, among which he can spend a lifetime without ever needing a peregrine for greater fulfilment.

A Falconers' Field Day in Yorkshire. One of the most encouraging signs for the future of British falconry is the number of small groups of people getting together in various parts of the country to hold hawking meets.

Out of the eight birds in this most interesting picture, only two, the kestrels, are British birds. There is an important aspect to this: it shows that falconry can flourish in Britain without having recourse to the hard-pressed native hawk population.

One would expect to find a goshawk or two in such a group, when the skill and experience of the members allow them to make such an excellent job of the longwings in the picture. The luggers are common in India and have been described by Mr. Mavrogordato in his learned treatise *A Falcon in the Field* as 'an inferior alternative to the lanner'. This may well be an unfair stricture, because the lugger lives a different life from, and preys on less demanding quarry than, the peregrine or lanner.

The lugger is an excellent substitute for the peregrine; the falconer who can handle the lugger has no difficulty in getting the best out of a peregrine, should he ever want one.

In the back row on the left is Jim Senior, a young falconer with his kestrel, and his colleague, Graham Kenworthy, kneeling in front, also with a kestrel. These home bred birds, obtained locally, are the ideal introduction to the sport. They are cheaply and comparatively easily obtained, but their manning and training needs just as much care in its own way as does the training of a more demanding hawk. The principles are the same, but if early mistakes are made, the result, although very regrettable, is not so disastrous as it would be for Mr. Marcus Barker, standing at the back, next to Jim Senior, with his Bonelli's Eagle.

This most handsome bird is very much smaller than the better-known golden eagle and is a little more easily handled and better tempered. It is not so likely to indulge in the appalling and terrifying fits of temper of the golden eagle, who happily gives up eating for days on end, thereby putting himself completely beyond anyone's control. The Bonelli will give excellent flights at hare, rabbit and all other similar quarry, but it is definitely not a hawk for a beginner.

In front of Mr. Barker is Mr. Peter Nightingale with his North American red-tailed hawk, which, from its increasing popularity in Britain, is evidently a hawk which finds wide favour among falconers. It is really a buzzard, but shows none of the usual buzzard characteristics of timidity, lethargy and tiny feet. It will fly with considerable dash at rabbits and similar quarry.

At the back, by the wall, is Mr. Fred Holmes with his spotted eagle, an exotic hawk but by all accounts fairly manageable. In front of him is Mr. Jim Walsh with his crested mountain hawk eagle, another variety probably more powerful than the other comparatively small types of eagle.

Kneeling in front and standing on the extreme right are Mr. Sydney Moore and Mr. Harold Booth, each with a female lugger.

It shows much enterprise to acquire, man, train and enter such a varied mews of hawks. Falconry does not lack enthusiastic support in Yorkshire.

CHAPTER 3

One result of the difficulty to get hold of any sort of
hawk, other than a kestrel, is that more must be made
of the kestrel than in previous years. It must not be
looked upon as merely an elementary stage, a pre-
liminary before graduation to grown up hawks. Much
pleasure and a lot less worry can result from a well
trained kestrel than with a more exotic, temperamental falcon bought at great expense from foreign
parts, with all the present paraphernalia of permits and
import licences.

As we have seen, even the kestrel is not free from
the requirement of a licence, but this costs no more
than the stamp on the application envelope.

As soon as the licence arrives it is time to make
serious plans for the taking of a bird from the nest
which has been marked down with the co-operation
of the owner of the land, or someone entitled to act
for him in the matter of permission. On the licence
application form you have to state where you propose
taking the bird from, and by what means.

This depends, of course, whether you have your
eye on a particular nest in which young birds are, to
your knowledge, growing up fast, or whether you
have a mind to try to trap a wild bird and tame it, or
'man it', as it is called, and train it to fly for you.
During the nesting period, and for a couple of months
afterwards, it would not be right to try to trap an adult
bird, since you might well capture a hen bird who was
feeding young, or sitting on eggs and had just come
off for a breather. In such a case, the other adult of the
pair might take over the family work, but it would be
very wrong to bring this situation about deliberately.

Therefore, if your operations are to start in the
spring and early summer, you will decide on taking
an eyass or young bird from the nest at a suitable time.
On your application form you will accordingly write:
'Take from the nest', in the space for: 'Means of
taking'.

With luck, the nest you have in mind will be reasonably accessible, since it is important to be able to
observe the progress of growth of the young occu-
pants. For they cannot, of course, be taken too young,
otherwise you will have a lot of unnecessary trouble

There would not be many volunteers to take this
eagle away from her quarry.

M. Pierre Branda's peregrine falcon, Lady,
photographed by M. François Merlet, a split
second before the flight, as reported
in *Chasse au Vol* 'se termina par
buffetage et prise d'un coq faisan'.

feeding. The parents are the best at this job, and they should be left to do it in peace.

Then what is the best stage? It is a matter of opinion, but many people would think it was best not to take the bird from the nest at all. If the bird is going to spend much of its time flying and catching things for you, it will have to learn how to do this, since instinct can only take it part of the way. And who better to give this extremely specialized and important instruction than the parent birds?

This means catching a bird after it has left the nest naturally, and has been at large for a few weeks learning the way of a kestrel from the example of its parents.

There are snags here. It is obviously much easier to climb up an easy tree, dip one's hand into a nest of young birds, pick out the biggest and most robust looking, slip it into a small fishing basket or some such container slung round the waist, climb down and return home. You are in business already.

If you are to catch a bird that is only seen rarely as it flits about a wood or hovers tentatively over fields and hedges, getting stronger every day, you have further to go before you can get a hawk on to your fist.

But you will certainly have a better hawk, certainly healthier to begin with, more skilful and imbued with that indefinable quality associated with a battle with nature surmounted the hard way. The obvious drawback is – can you catch such a hawk? Can you guarantee to trap one at all?

The other way, you at least have a hawk to work on, even if it does lack this indefinable something which the other displays. If you decide on the eyass out of the nest, give it the best chance by waiting until the very last moment before it is about to fly out of reach. The young bird, as soon as it is ready to walk off the nest, will try a few tentative steps along the neighbouring branches of the tree round the nest. From this exercise he gets his name of 'brancher'. This is the stage to catch him. It needs a little judgement not to scare all the branchers away so that they fall about by the nearby trees, getting lost or perhaps grounded and becoming a prey to dogs and cats – I once found the remains of a young kestrel beside a fox's earth. Most people will not risk the bird escaping and will take him before he starts being so adventuresome.

But supposing the decision is made to take the young bird after he has had a month's practical flying and catching for himself. You may be able to find out where he is roosting. If you are lucky enough to do so, you may then mark him down. Return at dead of night with a ladder of the necessary length, a particularly powerful torch and one other piece of equipment. This is simple but important and, in addition, should always be kept handy in case an escaped hawk has to be captured which will not return home by normal means. It is a bamboo or other light cane, four or five feet long. Two small holes are made about half an inch and one and a half inches from one end, drilled so as not to split the cane.

To this is fixed a noose, made preferably of heaviest gauge nylon cast, with a slip knot like a snare, and a stop knot tied in it to prevent it closing entirely. The slip knot must be loose and not one which will tighten when pulled on.

The procedure is obvious and in theory quite straightforward. Shine the torch in the hawk's face and keep it there. It is easier with an assistant, but it naturally depends how accessibly the bird is perching. Place the ladder as quietly as possible against, if possible, not the tree itself on which the hawk is perched, but one within reach, to save banging the perch. Climb carefully within the cane's distance, reach up and slip the noose over the hawk's hunched head. With any luck the action of the light, together with the stumbling, banging, dropping of torch, mutterings and other manifestations of something being afoot, will tend to make the hawk stick out her neck, an easier target than if she obstinately stays asleep.

A quick yank with the cane will bring her tumbling into your lap, the assault being too sudden to allow her time to grip the perch, and the stop in the noose preventing you decapitating her. This is, or rather used to be, a great way of pulling pheasants off their roosts, when a very long jointed light pole was substituted for a short cane. This was a specially made piece of equipment, and hardly worth the falconer

Capturing or recapturing a wild or lost hawk at dusk with the aid of chloroform or sulphur and a bee smoker. Dead of night is the safest time, if the hawk has been tracked down at nightfall, and a torch in the hawk's face is a help. It is worth going to inordinate lengths to retake a hawk which is rapidly going wild, since her chances of survival in a populated area are small and, once contact between hawk and falconer has been lost, it is essential to stop at nothing to get her back.

preparing, for all the times he might use it. But it certainly saves the performance of dragging a ladder through a wood in the middle of the night.

Here is another apparatus which I have used, not only for capturing a wild roosting hawk, but also for recovering a lost hawk which is killing for itself early every morning and therefore rapidly reverting to the wild. It is complicated but has been marvellously successful on occasion.

You need a bee-smoker, which is one of those small bellows contraptions into which beekeepers put a piece of lighted rolled corrugated paper, snap the funnel shut, and puff out varying amounts of smoke over bees which appear unduly menacing. If an old smoker cannot be acquired, a new one will have to be bought and this could cost up to £3. Then a number of jointed, hollow, very light metal tubes must be obtained in lengths perhaps of three feet or so. A half inch diameter is ample. The funnel of the bee-smoker must then be restricted and reinforced to take the first length of tube, which will probably be aluminium. This is the least difficult to obtain and the most satisfactory, being the lightest. Sometimes the jointed poles sold by such firms as Gale and Polden of Reading for poking out grey squirrels' dreys or pigeons' nests are hollow. These serve very well.

Instead of rolled corrugated paper, a piece of damp rag or sacking is soaked in a very strong solution of sulphur, with a little oil of any sort added. After being well soaked, and thoroughly impregnated with the sulphur, the rag is put out to dry, after which it is ready for use, and can be kept almost indefinitely in a tin with a lid.

It will smoulder when lit round one side, frayed out a bit if necessary. Put it in the canister, shut down the lid, joint up the rods to the required length near the scene of intended action, and come as quietly as possible below the unsuspecting hawk. It is very important not to bang a branch with the waving, smoking tube or the hawk may get such a fright as to fly off and keep flying until daylight. Gentle puffing as near beneath the hawk's head as possible will soon stupefy her, provided the wind is not too strong, and

Mr. David Gosmore's adult female goshawk, displaying her wings in majestic fashion, looks well capable of living up to her formidable name of Evil Hands. Her display also shows to very good advantage the conformation of the shortwing.

Mr. M. P. Clowes's red-tailed hawk 'mantles' defensively over a heavy Cheshire hare which she has just taken. A hawk needs a stout heart as well as strength to catch and hold a full-grown hare. Red has become an expert, supporting the growing popularity of these fine American hawks.

Right: a study of an adult female goshawk — this one belongs to Mr. David Gosmore.

in a moment she will topple unharmed into your waiting arms.

On the last occasion I operated this advanced technological apparatus, I gave the heavily blinking and panting bird, after her recapture, several shots of neat oxygen from a small aerosol-type container, but this may have been an unnecessary refinement.

As an alternative to sulphur, several falconers have told me they have used cotton wool damped with chloroform. This is a little more difficult to use, certainly dangerous, but probably more efficient. A Scottish falconer who tried this single-handed one night was discovered unconscious below the tree, with his stupefied hawk lying on top of him. Both recovered to continue their hawking careers.

But obviously, chloroform should only be used with great discretion: an overdose can easily kill both man and hawk.

If all this seems too complicated, or you are unable to take steps to get a bird yourself, which is far the most satisfying way of starting a practical interest in the subject, you may be reduced to watching the advertisement columns of suitable magazines. You may be lucky enough to hear of some other enthusiast who, for some reason or another, wishes to give up his hawk. Such a bird may be half trained, or fully trained, or in a state where an untutored beginner has 'had a go', been able to make nothing of it, and now wants to get rid of it.

You will need to know what you are getting before you take on one of these. The bird may have learnt habits which would perhaps take an experienced falconer weeks to eliminate before the hawk can get down to disciplined flying. Some of these habits may be so deeply ingrained that the time and effort to bring it round might not be worth it. On the other hand, it might have been properly treated and gently trained and be without vice of any sort. If it is healthy as well, you might find yourself with a hawk on which all the hard work of 'manning' (making used to people and

Mr. J. M. Buckner, Treasurer of Clwb Hebogwyr
Cymru, the Welsh Hawking Club, with his
red-tailed hawk, Sioux, now eight years old.

An alabaster goshawk keeps serene watch over the High Street at Valkenswaard, the headquarters of the Dutch hawk-trapping business carried on for many generations, latterly by the Mollen family until the end of the 1920s. Hawks were sold to falconers all over Europe, particularly to Britain, where Adriaan Mollen, the last great professional trapper, supplied passage hawks, chiefly peregrines, to order, for £3 or £4.

things) has already been done. From such a stage you might progress rapidly to flying the hawk free, and perhaps catching quarry.

But many people would frown on such a course for a beginner. To know the subject thoroughly it is best to go through it all from the very beginning and not take short cuts. In years gone by there would be no excuse for a learner taking such a course. Nowadays it must be looked at a little differently.

We all know the old saying about a bird in the hand and with the present state of affairs one might wait for many months before having a chance of getting hold of a bird of any sort. Who would blame a beginner today for taking whatever he could get, even if the bird seemed half trained or in some other way not the most desirable to start work on?

I would not complain about such actions. The important thing would be not to start with a species of bird which was wholly unsuited to a beginner. These are liable to come from the advertisements of bird dealers, zoos and others which is the big danger in buying a hawk in this manner. All sorts of hawks are obtained from abroad by dealers, and many beginners are tempted to buy one since it seems to be all they are going to be able to get.

Many strange exotic birds are offered from time to time, sometimes so unusual that one has to thumb through obscure lists before finding out what they really are. There are now more restrictions on the importing of birds than before, so these situations are not so likely to arise. Also, some of the exporting countries are tightening up on the hitherto unrestricted exporting of their hawks and other birds. For the dumping of poisonous chemicals goes on unchecked in many countries abroad.

But the learner falconer cannot concern himself with that. He is only brought into active awareness of the problem of that now overworked and self-conscious phrase 'environmental pollution' when he finds the supply of native hawks drying up, and he is forced to subscribe to appropriate magazines for any chance of getting a hawk.

The organized clubs, however, are often able to

Far left: a Spy cartoon of the Hon. Gerald Lascelles, 1849–1927, who was manager of the Old Hawking Club from 1872. The club was the predecessor of the present British Falconers' Club, subscription for which was £25 in 1890. The Hon. Gerald Lascelles was the author of the Badminton Library section on falconry, the first half of the volume dealing with coursing. A surveyor by profession (being Deputy Surveyor of the New Forest for 34 years), he was a crack shot as well as a great falconer. He was proud of his achievements when he ran the Old Hawking Club, although not everyone shared his opinion of his success. 'I believe I may say without arrogance that we can show the best sport that falconry has seen since the death of the Loo Hawking Club,' (the great Dutch Club), he said.

Left: the Mogul Emperor Jehangir, 1596–1627, son of Akbar the Great ascended the throne at Delhi in 1605 and is seen here seated with his favourite goshawk. This reproduction of a painting, now in the possession of Mr. H. C. Clifton, came from the Palace at Burdwan of the Maharajadhiraja Bahadur of Burdwan after the government of West Bengal assumed ownership of the palace in 1954.

Below left: the hawkers of Ko-i-staun. A print from Rattray's Afghanistan shows the valley of Kabul and the mountains of the Hindu Kush.

get small supplies of suitable hawks from abroad, and these may be rationed out to deserving members who apply for them. This is one more incentive for anyone wanting to take up hawking to apply for membership of a club. Quite apart from the value of his support in swelling the number of members, thereby strengthening the hand of the club in government or parliamentary negotiations, the member may have a good chance of being allotted a suitable hawk.

There would probably be nothing under £20 from club sources, but there might equally well be nothing under that sum from any other supply. From my own postbag over the past year or so, I know that much more money is being paid for what can only be described as winged pigs in pokes: an Indian kestrel, very tattered, having been kept in a small wire netting-fronted box, and apparently missing nearly every feather, £25. A lanner (an Eastern hawk rather like a peregrine), £35; some queer type of eagle, which died within a day or so, £50. This is the sort of money that complete beginners are somehow raising, which shows a lot of confidence and a real urge to get into hawking.

Clubs should do all they can to collect these people in, show them the right way to go with every encouragement, particularly by putting them in touch with the nearest practising falconer, and thereby prevent them spending absurd sums on equally absurd birds – to the great gain of often unscrupulous and ill-qualified dealers.

Many would-be beginners are lost to falconry through lack of knowing how to get in touch with others enjoying the same sport. I am often surprised and delighted to come across someone who has made great progress on his own without knowing or caring about anyone else in the falconry world. This is the excellent enthusiast who has won through, despite all difficulties. But the physical deterrents to acquiring a bird have caused many a learner, who might have proved of great value as a club supporter and upholder of falconry in general, to fall by the wayside. There is little excuse for this if he takes the trouble to find out the address of a club.

CHAPTER 4

Hawking is not a spectator activity. It is, of course, very exciting to be able to watch an expert fly a hawk, and no opportunity should ever be missed of doing so. One learns not only from the established falconer, but from the first efforts of the earliest beginner. I go long distances to see people make their very first hawking steps – provided I am invited. Nothing is worse than friends crowding round, unasked, urging one to: 'see if she'll fly', or to: 'give her one more try'. One should never be persuaded to do this. Hawking is essentially a lonely sport, the falconer and his hawk progressing together towards what is surely one of the most exciting relationships a human being can establish with a non-human.

This can be on a very modest scale. It often goes no further than the distant contact established between a provider of food and the ready recipient. It is a mistake to think that all hawks get fond of their owners, or partners as I prefer to think of them, in the manner of dogs.

The abrupt fashion in which an escaped hawk can sever all previous relationship with her partner without apparently the slightest qualm or backward look over her shoulder, comes as a sad shock to many falconers as their pet of many months, or even years, streaks for the horizon, never to be seen again.

With most combinations of hawk and hawker, tolerance is the main theme of the working partnership built up between the two. There is no doubt that some hawks do go much further than this. They really do seem fond of their partner, certainly recognize them from a distance among strangers, even chirp and fluff when spoken to by the loved one. I like to think my own gos, with me now for 13 years, has a certain feeling towards me which might be bordering on affection. She certainly talks a lot to me in her own way when spoken to, and allows great liberties to be taken with her, which favours she does not accord to other people. She has other very recognizable and apparently friendly ways of conveying some feeling towards me, and will sometimes call to me from a long way off.

But I have no illusions that if she were loose for a

The epitome of disciplined falconry — a superlative falcon superbly flown by Dr. Heinz Meng, a leading American falconer. Here, his 1965 passage peregrine falcon is shown after being adjudged the winner of a meet held in South Dakota in the autumn of 1971. The standard of American falconry today is very high. The most exhaustive research and experiment is carried out, resulting in a degree of expertise almost certainly unsurpassed in hawking history.

Mrs. Fran Hamerstrom's eagle, Nancy, comes to the fist, below. Mrs. Hamerstrom, the noted Wisconsin falconer, is extremely strong and brave to cope with such a bird. In the picture opposite, Nancy is just about to come to grips with a fox with which she is used to dealing rapidly and severely. But the difficulty is what to do when Nancy is standing on the dead fox. She does not want to eat it, certainly does not want anyone else to have it, and will sit over it for hours on end.

week or two, she might easily forget she had ever known me. I hope not to have to put this to the test.

Eagles sometimes seem to become very fond of their owners. But anyone who uses an eagle for regular free flying needs to be someone special. D. J. Cullen, writing warmly about his Austrian golden eagle, Taro, seven foot wing span, $9\frac{1}{2}$lbs. weight, reports: 'I think she is the most affectionate bird I have ever had, always pleased to see me, and she never calls to anyone else: she is very well mannered and will never snatch food.'

This sounds very nice. But what does Mr. Cullen say a few paragraphs later? Reluctantly, he goes on: 'She *can* get quite nasty. I have had her hanging on to my backside when I turn to put quarry in the bag: she has torn my clothes and cut and scratched me, but seldom done me much damage.' Just how far can affection go?

Most falconers would prefer to be able to sit down in comfort at the end of the day and do without such expressions of fondness.

There is no doubt that most eagle owners become devoted to their huge partners. There are several people flying them today who have great success with them and can at least come to some working arrangement with them. It may be unfair to disparage these partnerships, and I would not like to upset any of my eagle-owning friends. But an eagle is definitely not for a beginner.

Do not be persuaded by their magnificence or apparent gentleness. They can easily fast for several days, which makes them exceptionally difficult to control through their feeding. They are accustomed to standing quietly for very long periods. This does not mean they are taking a kindly view of life in general or of you in particular. It may just be a state of contemplative torpor. When they decide to bestir themselves, padded clothes and a fencing mask may not be enough. Once on the wing, flying free, it can be a memorable sight. But trouble starts again when you try to remove the eagle's kill.

A friend who has seen the wild Turkestanis flying black Caucasian eagles at fox and wolf from horseback reports that the casualty rate among horses, riders and general spectators, not to mention attendant dogs, was almost as high as among the intended quarry. This sounds bad enough. But the effect of a loose and extremely cross golden eagle flying down a crowded English village street at shoulder level has to be seen to be believed. Needless to say, it is not an experience I would like to repeat.

What other birds are there available these days?

We have seen that the kestrel can normally be obtained without too much difficulty, always provided the proper licence has been granted. Many people take kestrels, or receive them as gifts when picked up in the wild, without caring a fig for the licensing arrangements. Do not be persuaded to ignore this licensing. If you do receive a bird which someone has found or inadvertently trapped, keep and look after the bird, but write then to apply for a licence, stating that you already have the bird.

This regularizes the situation and prevents the law coming into disrepute through being widely ignored. It may not be a law with which everyone agrees, but the more falconers adhere to it the better say in these matters the hawking fraternity will have.

After you have got the kestrel to fly free, to hover on demand by use of the lure, and perhaps to fly prettily at sparrows, starlings or other quarry, you will feel the need for further progress towards a hawk which means real business – which can take a rabbit, hare or pheasant, or whatever quarry you may have a chance of flying at. This includes rooks, magpies and all birds and animals at which it is legal to fly a hawk. If your hawk flies and takes a protected bird, you can hardly be held to blame. The interpretation of this section of the Bird Protection Act must of necessity be very elastic.

Unless you have regular access to open country for flying a hawk, there is no doubt that the bird to aim for is a goshawk. In under a month, the male or female can be trained to take all manner of quarry for you. They are not fussy about food and will eat almost anything provided for them.

The problem of obtaining one is much the same as

A hawking meet in Russia.

for other hawks. They will have to come from abroad where they are not uncommon. In Germany, a previously good source of supply, their numbers do appear to be dwindling. They are not protected by law from overkeen game preservers and game farmers, while in Finland and other parts of Scandinavia they are known, from Government returns, to be destroyed in thousands. The difficulty is to contact someone who, rather than wringing a trapped goshawk's neck, would put it in a basket and send it to you by air.

One way is to apply through membership of a hawking club. A club secretary will have contacts in other countries and can usually arrange for a small number of good birds to be selected and sent over safely in a consignment, or singly from time to time. But it would have to be realized that established members would have first call on these, and that anyway a bird would not be made available to anyone who had not been known to have served some adequate apprenticeship by training at least a kestrel, or otherwise established his capability to receive a hawk.

This means that a comparatively new falconer who may feel himself ready to tackle the greater responsibility of a goshawk can sometimes never find one. The prospect of waiting month after month to move up the hierarchy of a club until he qualifies for an imported hawk will not appeal to him.

There are some steps he can take on his own. Apart from studying advertisements as mentioned before, he can write to the Commercial Attaché of, for instance, Finland or Sweden, whose address is found in the London telephone book. He asks for the names of any game farms which the Embassy is good enough to provide him with. They will usually provide a name or two. It is then up to him to write to the director of the game farm, explaining what he wants to do and inviting the director's co-operation in sending a hawk over to Britain.

This sometimes works very well, and sometimes does not work at all. It is not easy at such long range to get such an enterprise organized. You will have to offer to pay for the trouble involved at the game farm:

£5 seems usually ample to cover this, although of course every case may vary. The transport can easily come to £20 by the time everything is paid for. From further afield, it will of course be proportionately more and it is naturally important to find out from the national airline office what charges are likely to be incurred.

Make sure that the bird is not sent off until you have received your licence from the relevant Ministry Department, in London or Edinburgh. The Customs will not release the bird to you without production of your licence. If you do not have it, the Customs are in a quandary which may easily result in the bird's death, since it cannot be put indefinitely into an animal hostel at the airport with any good chance of survival.

This same procedure applies if you wish to import any bird from any other part of the world. Make sure everything is ready for receiving the bird, and that delay at the airport is as little as possible. The journey is, of course, a great shock to a wild bird, especially to a hawk. Quietness and rest are the first essentials; it is useful for the ending of a noisy and terrifying time to be associated in the hawk's mind with the arrival of his partner, the falconer.

There will not nowadays be much choice, if any, about what stage of life your bird will be in when she comes to you. Years ago it was possible to specify what was wanted, either *eyass* (taken from the nest), *passager* (a bird which has left the nest, and is 'on passage', or migration for the first time, not yet having acquired its adult plumage), or *haggard* (a fully adult bird taken at any time).

Some people would agree that the finest bird to train is a haggard. She has learnt her trade most thoroughly in the best and most natural way, she rarely has fits of temper or screams endlessly, like some eyasses do, and she is more gentle and amenable once manned and trained. She will probably take longer, however, and be more difficult.

On the other hand, it is possible that a lost haggard reverts more quickly to the wild, and there is therefore less chance of getting her back. But this is not an opinion accepted by everyone.

The Hon. Mrs. John Morris feeds her husband's eyass sparrowhawk, Elanna, on a magpie she has just taken. As an example of what a well-entered and properly handled sparrowhawk can do, Elanna, Irish for 'my pet', has a formidable record. In three weeks she caught and killed 12 magpies, four of them in one day, and four moorhens. It is not easy to bring a sparrowhawk to this pitch and maintain her there, and it is certainly not a bird for a beginner.

Right: a young eyass.

If it is to be your first important hawk, and you have the choice, it would be wise to choose an eyass. Often enough time has passed, and you have built up a bit of experience of your own and have seen a few other people handling their birds, and you will be able to make your own opinion about these matters.

Failing a goshawk, which you should certainly not tackle until you have handled one or two other hawks to your satisfaction, you could try for a sparrowhawk.

This will be hard to get, unless you happen to be in a district where they have been doing particularly well. A licence to take one is wanted of course, on application to The Home Office or Scottish Department, as said before.

There are different sorts of sparrowhawk abroad, in Africa and Australia in particular. The British bird is particularly charming. Within a couple of weeks you will have the sparrowhawk darting from your fist and, we hope, coming back on demand. It is now legitimate to fly her at her natural quarry which is black-birds, one of the country's most numerous birds. She will also fly at almost anything else on wings that is not too big. Her courage and brilliance in flight makes her one of the most exciting birds.

Sparrowhawks are still regularly trapped and destroyed, despite their legal protection, and no one hears anything about it.

If you can find someone who is doing this, it is not usually difficult to persuade him to let you have the next one for a consideration. You should then apply for a licence, stating that you have rescued the bird from destruction. It is not necessary to say who you got it from. If you do disclose this, the result may be that every sparrowhawk captured in the future will be destroyed in secret, whatever the illegality, and you will have no chance of getting one. These are the sorts of occasions when a little tact gets the best results for all concerned, including the sparrowhawk. If this almost completely unenforceable law is adhered to, which is designed to keep the maximum number of protected birds – in this case the sparrowhawk – alive, it very often has the effect of achieving exactly the opposite result.

It is therefore the duty of every falconer or would-be falconer to intervene as often as possible to save the life of a hawk whenever occasion arises.

The sparrowhawk has very long, delicate, thin legs. It is easy to get one broken, particularly to begin with when she may be wild and 'bates' off her perch, jerking violently away in an effort to fly. It is easy for her to throw a fit and die: she is not a simple bird to look after at first. But do not be discouraged if a sparrowhawk is the only bird which is likely to come your way, provided, as with the others, you have served your apprenticeship with a kestrel. The same principles will apply basically with all birds. But some will give you more latitude for mistakes or accidents than others.

It is difficult to say which hawk generally has the most delightful personality. The falconer will probably get very fond of any bird he has, although there have been notable exceptions to this.

A buzzard could be considered to begin with. It has

An adult peregrine falcon, powerful, heavy and perfectly mannered, gets ready to take off some summer fat before the game season starts.

the advantage of not being so impossible to find in Britain as any of the other hawks, and although it will not do anything very sensational in the way of catching quarry, it will at least respond well to manning, and will train without much difficulty.

It will get the early enthusiast into the way of a hawk. When he thinks he knows it all and finds the buzzard not exciting enough, he can return it to the wild from where it came. This is called 'hacking back' and is a recognized procedure described later. It is very important not just to turn a hawk loose when she is no longer to be kept with you. It is a careful process designed to ensure that the hawk is fully able to look after itself, and becomes gradually wild again – or wild for the first time if it was an eyass taken from a nest.

It cannot necessarily look after itself at once. It is essential, therefore, that no one turns a hawk loose without ensuring that it can do so, as far as it is humanly possible to guarantee.

A merlin can give great pleasure and can be almost fully trained in a week. But again its numbers have decreased disastrously in the past few years, and it is as good as unobtainable today. No beginner should contemplate acquiring one. Perhaps in years to come, it will be numerous enough for anyone who wishes to train and work larks with these marvellous little birds to be able to get one. Red-headed merlins are obtainable from India, but they are still not a beginner's bird.

It is now legal to fly a merlin at a lark. The flight is one of the most exciting which it is possible to enjoy. In theory, the lark rises straight up in its usual fashion: the merlin, then slipped, flies round and round the lark in circles, ringing as it is called, trying to get higher than the lark in order to put in a stoop at it.

With a strong lark and a determined merlin, it is possible to lie on one's back and watch them almost out of sight as they climb higher and higher. Soon the lark either suddenly gives up the struggle and drops like a stone right to the ground where it takes cover in a tuft of grass – once even in my own coat left lying on the ground – or the merlin gives up and comes sailing shamefacedly back to the lure or fist.

From this it can be seen that the lark usually escapes.

The eyass merlin, although tiny, is a longwing falcon. Her dark brown eye, as opposed to the gold of the shortwing sparrowhawk, goshawk and others, is plainly discernible, as is also the notch in her beak, another characteristic of the longwing, and used for the quick breaking of neck bones of her unfortunate quarry.

Trained hawks help to keep RAF runways clear of
birds which are a danger to aeroplanes.

It is customary to hack a merlin back to the wild after a season's lark hawking with her, but she can be kept over the winter with luck and care. It is doubtful whether a merlin kept this way ever flies so well as a fresh caught bird.

But at the moment this tends to be more of an academic point for discussion by the growing number of falconers and enthusiasts for whom 'the old days' were always so much better in every way. In many directions, of course, the old days of hawking *were* better. There were many more birds to choose from, they were far easier to obtain, and the costs were a great deal lower.

In still older days, there were fewer fences, and general enclosures, and it was easier to get about the country, with fewer people, roads, houses and less traffic in the way.

But we are not so concerned here with how splendid everything used to be. We have to take the situation as it is, how it will be, and get the best out of whatever hawking can be done now. The situation is far from desperate, although the plight of such birds as the British peregrine may certainly be in that category and getting worse.

Having practically dismissed the merlin as one more unobtainable, what does remain?

The hobby certainly does not remain. Too rare even to contemplate, the hobby is one of the smallest hawks, of great beauty and speed with very long, thin wings. Few people have ever seen a wild one chasing moths or dragonflies with the speed and manoeuvrability of a swift. There may well be fewer than 100 pairs left in Britain today, but the number has probably never been very great.

Most falconers hope to possess a peregrine one day. The chances of doing so are small. Licences, at the time of writing, are not being granted to take a home bred bird. Any home bred bird in anyone's possession apart from those allowed to Service Air Stations for clearing runways from birds likely to obstruct the aeroplanes, can only be there illegally. The policy of not granting these licences, even to recognized falconers, has been under heavy fire and has been widely blamed for a

An impressive picture of Mr. David Gosmore's
goshawk caught in the act of landing on her perch.

share of the responsibility in the peregrine's decline in Britain today.

When it was legal to take an eyass peregrine, established falconers often had their pet eyries in parts of the country where they cosseted the peregrines, with the active assistance of local people. The falconer was well known in the district, and he was expected to come every year and take the few birds he needed. Local intruders were more strictly watched and often given short shrift if they turned out to be egg stealers or robbers of the nestlings. The whole system tended to protect the peregrine pairs in each district.

But now, with the loyal law-abiding falconer obliged to give up his annual quest, the stage has been turned over to the roving bird dealer, or occasional maverick falconer, belonging to no club and not caring where or how he gets his birds, or what happens to the future of falconry, as long as he is all right himself. This is an irresponsible attitude which can do nothing but harm to the whole of falconry in general and to the birds in particular.

With the small numbers of enthusiasts involved in falconry in Britain, and with the legal future of the whole sport not by any means assured, it is doubly important that no one, beginner or old hand, should involve himself in doubtful dealings which, if publicised, may help those wishing to ban hawking.

The strength of the hawking clubs has been the disciplined approach to this whole matter by their members, making it all the more important that a beginner should seek to ally himself to a club. It is equally important that the club should help the beginner and not turn him away with the impression that there are too many people already interested in hawking nowadays.

The peregrine is obtainable on rare and costly occasions from the Far East, Canada, America, India and the Middle East. But anyone who has an opportunity of getting a peregrine must make sure that he is thoroughly ready and fit to receive such an honoured and lofty partner.

If he has learnt his job with the kestrel and maybe with some other hawk as well, he has nothing to fear in the handling of a peregrine. But it behoves him to be doubly careful not to destroy such a comparatively rare and beautiful bird, and a hawk for which most experienced falconers in the world would gladly give a great deal.

In certain markets in the Far East, peregrines and many other varieties of bird are to be found being offered for sale to the local population for eating. Peregrines are particularly sought after, people paying the equivalent of several pounds for the very small meat a peregrine would provide. They are rumoured to have aphrodisiac properties, which may account for such a high price when destined for the kitchen.

Anyone who is able to buy a peregrine or other hawk and save her from such a fate should certainly not hesitate to do so, whether a beginner or not. It must be preferable to be mishandled by an inexperienced falconer than to be made into a Chinese curry.

The peregrine must have wide open spaces in which to be flown. It is disgraceful to keep a peregrine as a pet bird, permanently tethered to her block. It is very doubtful whether zoos should be allowed to keep peregrines and some other birds in permanent cages. It is not, of course, done very often.

The main point about the peregrine is the great stoop, from perhaps 1,000 feet, which she puts in, driving down on to the fleeing partridges, grouse, and even rook or other quarry, at speeds estimated in some cases up to 180 m.p.h., but more likely to be in the region of half that, and from 50 feet up or less.

She strikes the quarry with her foot closed, like a fist. The combined force is often enough to smash the quarry into the ground. It used to be thought that only the hind toe of the hawk was used, and that the quarry was slashed on the back of the head with this needle tip. But this is almost certainly not the case, since the toe itself could never sustain being struck against any object at that speed. In addition, the quarry which one picks up after a successful stoop has never, to my knowledge, been found to have the fearful gash on its back or head which such an assault would give.

But it does not do to be too dogmatic about any of these questions. There have been arguments over such

Top right: a tundra tiercel, showing the head colouring which is very typical of the tundra.

Top far right: a pure white gyrfalcon, caught in the act of 'rousing' or fluffing up her feathers which is a sign of well-being. Held beside her is a tiercel Peale's falcon.

Below right: a five-week-old kestrel. It is not easy to tell male from female, since the difference in sizes is not marked.

Below far right: a tiercel lugger.

points for generations past, and doubtless there will remain a good proportion of flat-earthists among falconers in the future.

Another unobtainable hawk is the gyrfalcon, the great white hawk of the Arctic, also called a Greenland and Iceland falcon. Another version comes from Norway, of darker colour and not so spectacular as the others, and yet more from Alaska.

This would doubtless be the pinnacle of hawking birds, with all the power and speed of the falcon and more besides, including greater weight. But so few people have ever flown them satisfactorily that one rather suspects they are not manageable and would be a great deal more trouble – and expense – than they could be worth.

I believe that they have been sought after so avidly over the centuries chiefly for their truly amazing beauty. To see a Greenland falcon slipped into a clear blue sky, or to watch her stooping at unimaginable speeds towards her quarry, is a sight really to take the breath away. Not many people have ever seen it, or are likely to do so. Export from Greenland is now finally forbidden by law, which does not of course mean that they will not appear in the outside world. One was shot in Anglesey in the summer of 1972, but this would probably have been a Norwegian bird, or one escaped from some aviary.

They are more prone to various obscure diseases than most other hawks, but since their acquisition is so unlikely, it is hardly worth going into any detail. A few people have experience of gyrfalcons and have achieved great success with them, notably Mr. Ronald Stevens, one of the foremost falconers, both in practice and theory, of modern times. In America, the gyr has been more readily obtainable, and many have been and are being flown with brilliant results. But for the beginner, this is one more not to be considered, even if it were to become available.

It would be small encouragement to extol the virtues of a particular breed of hawk, implying that it was the only bird worth using and finish by saying that you could never get hold of one.

Fortunately, there are other hawks which come near

The prairie falcon in both pictures below belongs to Herr Walter Crammer of the Austrian Hawking Club. These North American hawks, similar to peregrines but lightish brown all over, are often extremely difficult to handle. They can fly well, but are very temperamental at times and should be left to the experienced falconer. Many are flown with great success in America.

Right: Mr. John Morris casts off his eyass saker falcon, Farah, who is the mother of the 1971 hybrid tiercel in the picture on page 149.

to a peregrine's performance which a newcomer to the sport is quite likely to be able to acquire. They are becoming increasingly popular in Europe: it is now more often possible to find a falconer who is passing his bird on for some perfectly adequate reason. It is also possible to import these birds from India and the Middle East, although the difficulty of getting contact with someone who can deal with the arrangements the other end remain formidable.

These are the hawks generally known in a block as Desert falcons, the lanners, laggars, luggers and sakers. The prairie falcon is similar in appearance to these superficially, but is a native of western North America, Mexico and western Canada. It is widely used in the States, and works very well in skilled hands.

To the unpractised eye, they can all look very much the same, although when seen together the colouring is very different. They all resemble the peregrine, and have much the same characteristics. Being longwing falcons with dark eyes, they fly from a height, and are

trained to 'wait on' above the falconer's head while game is produced for them to fly at. This is, of course, the opposite to the shortwinged, yellow-eyed hawks who fly direct at the quarry from the fist or perch.

They illustrate the great difference between the two sorts of falconry, the latter tending always to be called hawks and the others falcons – although falcon is a term strictly applied only to a female peregrine or female of the peregrine species in general. A female sparrowhawk does not get called a falcon, nor does a female kestrel, although she is one of the dark-eyed longwings. Anyone who called a female buzzard a falcon would cause some sniffs and raised eyebrows at any gathering of established falconers.

Sakers are fine birds, but not too easily managed. They are courageous and can be flown at any large quarry one is likely to find in Britain. They have certain training difficulties, and easily adopt bad habits such as carrying their kill away before you can get up to them. This is known, not unnaturally, as 'carrying',

and is a very difficult habit to break. Merlins are particularly susceptible, and indeed any hawk will quickly learn it if given the opportunity. The male saker is known as a sakret.

A lanner is an attractive bird without so many potential vices as a saker. She is a little smaller than the saker, and looks again very much like a peregrine. Since all these birds come from basically hot countries, they tend not always to be at their best in the British climate. The climate may account for the lanner's reputation for laziness. But it may not be that she is lazy so much as not liking the weather. She is probably slower, anyway, than the saker in flight and is happy to catch small rodents and other little animals and insects on the ground.

But she is a very desirable hawk to have, like the saker. Her largely buff-coloured head usually helps distinguish her from the peregrine saker and others. The saker is bigger than the peregrine, and the lanner about the same as the peregrine.

A laggar is an Indian falcon, about the same size as a peregrine, and the lugger another Indian variation.

Others one is likely to come across are the shahin, from India, the barbary falcon, also from the East, and a large variety of more or less obscure birds and their variants.

Any of the more exotic falcons can probably be trained quite satisfactorily, provided the climate is not too upsetting. But even if they do react unfavourably to the weather, they can usually be worked quite well provided, of course, they are not allowed to remain damp or get cold.

There are literally dozens of hawks from all over the world which find their way into dealers' hands in Britain, or into advertisements, which the intending falconer can make something of, provided as always that he has done his homework very thoroughly with his kestrel.

Some of the more curious birds may have hidden characteristics which only emerge during training. For this reason it is best to stick to a type of bird about which something is known, however vague. If nothing else were available, nor likely to be for the

Itza, my micrastur semi-torquatus, a collared forest falcon, was the most dreadful bird I ever took into partnership. Sent as a present from Peru for hare-hunting by a well-known American falconer friend, it can only have been intended as a bad joke. It was a perfect lesson in not trying exotic foreign hawks without knowing their habits and hawking capabilities. Merciful release for both of us, in the form of a fit by Itza, did not come for over two long years.

foreseeable future, there would be no harm in taking it on. But one has to be prepared for disappointments.

An American friend, a keen falconer, knowing that I wanted to concentrate on the catching of hares at the time, sent me a hawk from Peru which he said would be just the thing. It turned out to be a micrastur semi-torquatus, a collared forest falcon. Of vile temperament (Perthshire and Peru evidently have little in common) and most mean disposition, the hawk, whom I named Itza, would frequently run after me through the long grass on legs like a stork's and jump on my back. He never took his hawking seriously, occasionally gliding away down a valley at high speed just above the ground to land on some distant barnyard fowl too far away for me even to see.

After a couple of years' unhappy relationship, Itza threw a violent fit and expired. It was a blessed release for us both.

But it was a lesson not to take on exotic birds unless there is really nothing else. Air carriage has made it possible to bring all manner of birds to this country, so that the most surprising and, to most people, unheard of hawks are sometimes available. There are grey hawks, white hawks, black hawks, chanting goshawks, (do not be persuaded to take one of these even

as a gift – it is not an ordinary goshawk given to singing quietly in the mews of an evening), red goshawks, even doria's goshawk – there are enough hawks to fill a whole chapter just by listing their names.

Some of the less commonly known hawks, however, acquit themselves very well in Britain. One of the most popular in recent years is the red-tailed hawk of North America. Cooper's hawk, a North American bird closely resembling a peregrine, has been popular for hawking in North America and is sometimes seen over here, where she seems to work quite well.

It will be seen from all this that there is still plenty to choose from. But it is essential to go for an ordinary kestrel at first, even if it means waiting a bit longer before trying something more ambitious. No beginner should be tempted to take on one of the exotic foreign hawks until he has served his probation with his kestrel.

Once this probationship has been successfully undertaken, there is no reason why he should not cautiously graduate to whatever is available. He has to remember that a Middle Eastern or semi-tropical hawk has got to overcome the climatic change as well as the shock of capture and training, a double burden. The falconer must take account of this and make allowances.

58

Mr. Sydney Moore holds up his North American red-tailed hawk. The broad wing, more like that of a buzzard (which this hawk really is), contrasts strongly with the sickle-shape of the longwing falcons. The red tail is a most useful bird and, as well as being widely used in America, it is becoming increasingly popular in Britain.

CHAPTER 5

The few items of equipment needed to start with a hawk can all be bought nowadays, including, as we have seen, the hawk itself. Some addresses are given in the appendix at the end of this book. Reproduced on page 63 is the current price list of one of the oldest hawk merchants in Pakistan. His hoods and gloves are, of course, all Indian pattern, as opposed to European or a mixture of the two styles. Both Indian and Dutch hoods are illustrated on pages 126 and 127. A beginner has to make do with what he can get, but after a while he decides which pattern is best.

If he takes the matter at all seriously, he will want to dispense with as much bought equipment as possible. He will have a try at making all his own 'furniture', as hawking equipment is still called, and will hope to be able to take a wild hawk himself to go with it – in most cases, and most desirably, a native kestrel plucked from a nest or acquired in the manner already described. The necessary licence must not, of course, be forgotten.

The sport is so much a very personal relationship between the man – or woman – and the once wild bird, that the best can only be got out of it by contributing as much as possible, preferably everything, which can be made by hand.

These will all be described here and it is very much hoped that a learner will at least try his hand at making them before he gets a hawk. It is not easy, and as far as making a hood goes, most people – including myself – have never been able to make a properly fitting one. It has to be bought in the end, but this does not prevent one trying hard to be successful. As with tying a trout or salmon fly, it is much more satisfying to catch a fish on a fly or other lure which one has made oneself. This does not prevent the fisherman buying better made flies, minnows, spoons and other contraptions, but it is rewarding to know that provided he had enough time (always a good excuse for not doing something like this) one could, in fact, make whatever is necessary for taking the fish.

The hawking apparatus needed is not elaborate. Bells are essential. The ordinary person cannot possibly make these. They can be bought from some of

Dr. James Gow's ornate hawk eagle has just caught
a jack rabbit. An exotic, spectacularly beautiful
bird from Mexico and the Argentine, it is a hawk
not likely to come the way of most falconers.

A hawk, trained by Count Tosti of the Italian
Falconers' Club, clears a bird just in time from the
path of a plane at Torrejon in Spain.

Ch. Mohammed Din is a very long established hawk merchant in Lahore, Pakistan, and his bells are probably the finest now made. The prices quoted here are naturally subject to variation. Another dealer, in Calcutta, offers to provide any bird of prey 'from stock'. On inquiring what birds these were, and their prices, I received a list of elephants for sale in six different sizes, which all goes to show that buying a hawk from Eastern countries is not a simple affair.

the addresses at the end of the book. It is madness to fly a hawk free without bells.

If she is a shortwing, such as a goshawk or sparrow-hawk, she is likely, as soon as she has killed her quarry, to stand motionless over it, either on the ground or perhaps in a tree where she may have taken it, if guilty of the serious fault of 'carrying' it away. Her natural instinct will be to 'plume' or pluck it at once, if it is a bird, or to pull off a bit of fur if a rabbit or hare, and then eat her fill.

Should she be allowed to do this, she will see no point in returning to her partner for the time being, if at all. It is therefore extremely important to find her at once, supposing she has not been marked accurately down after the kill. A bell on each leg will give her away, since every jerk of her shoulders as she plucks her kill will give a tinkle of the bells. For a sparrow-hawk it is preferable to put one bell only on the tail, which is moved more often than the leg. A loose hawk can get stuck in a fence or branch – or even a bramble – by the bewits, or leathers, which tie the bell to the leg. But if the bell is on the tail, this danger is averted.

To attach the bell to the tail is not as difficult as it may sound, provided, that is, you have someone to hold the bird for you while you do it. If you have no helper, or no one who will help you willingly, you can dope the hawk with a drug called Equinal. This is available without prescription from most big chemists. Half a normal 100gm size tablet per pound weight of bird (and in proportion for smaller birds) will put the bird into a manageable coma for tail bell-ing, or indeed for any other operation for which the falconer needs a competent assistant and cannot get one.

I have never found this drug to have any side or after effects, and have occasionally used it for a car or train journey for a hawk which would otherwise be unduly distressed by the travelling.

But all drugs and medicines should only be used on hawks as a very last resort. The shock of a drug and the effort of combating its effect, as well as that of the condition for which the drug is being administered, frequently prove fatal to a hawk. One should be very

Phone : Grams : "BAZWALA"

Ch. Mohammad Din & Company
Manufacturers, Exporters & Importers, Hawk Merchant

Bankers :
The Chartered Bank
The Mall, Lahore.
United Bank Ltd.
S. D. Vault The Mall, Lahore.

PREM GALI No. 4
RAILWAY ROAD,
LAHORE
(W. Pakistan)

Ref. No.   Dated October 1972

PRICE LIST

				PER DOZEN Sterling - Pounds
BELLS				
Goshawk		....	....	£2.00
Merlin & Peregrine	(Female)			£3.00
Peregrine	(Male)			£2.00
Sparrow Hawk				£2.00
SWIVELLS				
Goshawk		....	....	£4.00
Merline & Peregrine	(Female)			£3.00
Peregrine	(Male)			£2.00
Sparrow Hawk				£2.00
HOODS				
Peregrine	(Female) (Plain)			£3.00
Peregrine	(Male)	„		£3.00
Goshawk		„ „		£3.00
Saker		„ „		£2.00
Sparrow h		„	....	£6.00
Goshawk	(Embroidered)			£6.00
Saker		„		£4.00
Sparrow Hawk		„		£6.00
Peregrine	(Female)	„		£6.00
Peregrine	(Male)	„		
GLOVES				
Five Fingers	(Plain)		....	£9.00
Three Fingers	„			£7.00
Two Fingers	„			£4.00
Five Fingers	(Embroidereb)			£34.00
Three Fingers	„			£28.00
Tow Fingers	„			£21.00
LASHES				
Goshawak				£11.00
Sparrow Hawk				£9.00
JANGOLIS				
Goshawk, or Merline				£2.00
GETUS				
Peregrine				£4.00

Note :-
1. Packing, Postage, Air Freight, forwarding charges will be extra.
2. All remittances should be made through. The Chartered Bank, The Mall, Lahore Pakistan. Or Australasia Bank Ltd, Shahalam Market Lahore Pakistan.
3. The season for these birds is from November to April only.
4. The availablity of Thise birds from November to April only.

The bells which are lightest and can be heard from the furthest distance are usually thought to be Indian, obtained from Lahore where they have been made for centuries, and recognisable by their waisted shape and thin metal. Their disadvantage, however, against the heavier Dutch or European bell, is that they wear out more quickly. The two below are only a year old and have worn so thin at the mouth that they have split and opened, and a piece of one has broken off.

chary of using all but the simplest and most natural remedies. In an emergency, or cases of extreme illness, one would naturally have no hesitation in trying whatever drug or medicine held out a chance of recovery. But if the illness has got that far, it is probably too late.

Bells are equally important for the high flying falcons, for the same obvious reasons. It is not always easy to spot your hawk in the air, especially if the country is rather wooded, or there are clumps or buildings to unsight you. The bells give away her position in flight from a surprisingly long way, especially if up wind. Half a mile is not too far for the sound of good bells to carry.

A longwing falcon, as opposed to the shortwinged hawk to which we have already referred, should not of course be flown in very wooded country. You are bound to lose her sooner or later if you do fly her in the wrong sort of country: she is out of sight in a moment, and if you cannot hear her bells you have no idea where she is. Other birds may, by mobbing her, give you a clue, but it does not make sense to risk it.

The bells are specially made, usually from very thinly beaten brass. The ordinary little bell for a cat's, dog's or baby's harness, is useless for the purpose. Ideally, the bells when on the legs of a hawk are a matched pair. Not matched to make exactly the same sound, but at least half a tone apart. The resulting dissonance when they are tinkled on the leg carries very much further than if they are level. Many people do not believe this, and think that trouble taken in matching bells is one more finicking detail pursued unnecessarily by pedantic purists.

This can easily be proved not to be the case. Let one person walk away from you with two pairs of bells, one in the same tone and one in dissimilar tones. As he tinkles two pairs alternately, you will very soon find the one pair becoming inaudible some good time before the other.

The bells made in Germany tend to be heavy in tone, as do those made in Holland and, very occasionally, in Britain. It is entirely a question of personal opinion and preference which is the best. The Indian ones, obtainable from Lahore, are reckoned to be the

Mr. John Morris's peregrine falcon, three-year-old Victoria, on the wing. This exceptional photograph shows clearly the open slits in the jesses which are potentially dangerous for a hawk flying quarry, as the slit can easily catch in a piece of fencing wire, twig or branch, causing the bird to get hung up. However, as Victoria is only flying to the lure, there is no danger of this.

best sounding bells, although being very thin they tend to wear out quickly with the action of the heavy little 'pea' inside. Most people will have to be satisfied with whatever bells they can get, and not be unduly fussy.

The manner of fixing them on, one on each leg above the jess with the small piece of leather already mentioned, called a 'bewit', is shown in the photograph on page 66. Also the tail fitting is shown. It is not too much to have a bell on the tail for, say, a goshawk, as well as on each leg. This minimizes the chance of her deliberately staying hidden in undergrowth, long grass or tree. Some hawks know very well that the bell gives them away, and are very cunning at remaining motionless on their quarry while the falconer searches everywhere.

The jess is the leather which the hawk has round each leg. Three sorts are illustrated in the photographs on pages 66 and 67. The first is the traditional method, which you can cut out quite easily, after experimenting a little in getting the distances correct between the slits to suit your particular bird. This method has been used since time immemorial. This does not mean to say we have to go on using it for all time to come, but it does mean that it is reliable and works.

It has one big disadvantage which is done away with by the second type. This can soon be explained when we realize that before the hawk can be flown free at her quarry, the long leash, or leather thong by which she is secured to her perch, and the swivel joint to which the jesses, one from each leg, are attached to this leash, all have to be taken off. The jesses used when she is at home on her perch should be replaced with jesses which have no slit in them.

The reason for flying her only in jesses with no slit is that this slit can easily catch in a piece of fencing wire or a twig or branch of a tree and the bird can then get hung up out of your sight and without your ever finding her. She dies very soon, either upside down of suffocation, or of sheer starvation, unable to get away.

This is a desperate thing to happen and inexcusable.

A traditional jess is shown here tied to a hawk's leg. The other end is tied to one loop of the swivel and the leash, up to three feet long, is threaded through the other loop of the swivel. The folded button on one end of the leash prevents the leash slipping through the swivel, and the other end of the leash is tied to the perch. The bell is secured to the hawk's foot by the bewit, and an unattached jess is shown lying to one side.

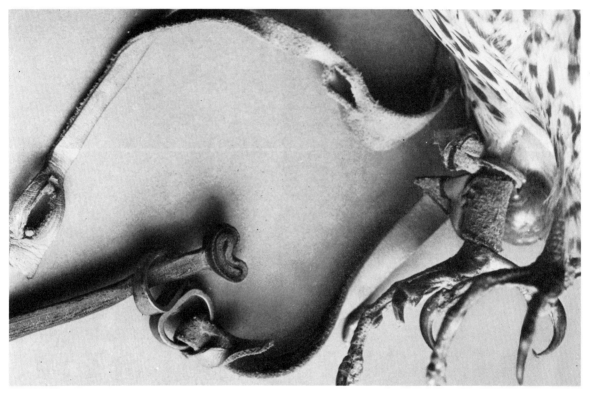

But it is surprising how many falconers take a chance and leave the permanent jesses on the whole time, simply because the business of changing jesses every time you want to fly the hawk becomes a chore. Also the hawk may resent the constant fiddling with her legs by a possibly not too practised hand, which might tend to upset her at a time when a calm approach is essential to success.

The jesses can be changed easily enough, but the fact remains that they do not get changed without fail every time, especially if, as is not unusual, they have not been kept properly supple with some form of leather grease or oil.

When the traditional type of jess is being used, and the hawk is being flown with jesses having the dangerous slit in them, the danger can be minimized by rolling the slit end between thumb and finger as soon as the jesses are taken off the swivel. This tends to keep the slits closed, or at least not gaping open, and not such a menace. It should become an automatic action whenever the swivel is disengaged from the traditional type of jesses.

To obviate this small chore, Major Guy Aylmer some years ago hit on the idea illustrated in the photograph on page 67. It is simple enough once you have discovered how to fix an eyelet on to two pieces of leather. You will soon find an ironmonger, saddler or sailmaker who stocks large eyelets and a very little experimenting will soon show you how to make a firm job of it.

When the hawk is at home, the long jesses with the normal slit thread easily through the eyelet, are secured to the swivel and this in turn is tied to the leash. When you take the bird out for exercise or flying, it is only necessary to unthread the jesses from the swivel. The bird then has two good long jesses by

Aylmeri jesses, showing a flying jess without slits and two forms of leg loop. The one on the left is an original, given to me by Major Guy Aylmer himself, the inventor. It has an additional rivet which makes it easier than the one on the right to put on the hawk's leg and take off, although it is rarely necessary to change it. There is also more room for putting on a small label with a telephone number in case the hawk gets lost and is discovered by a stranger.

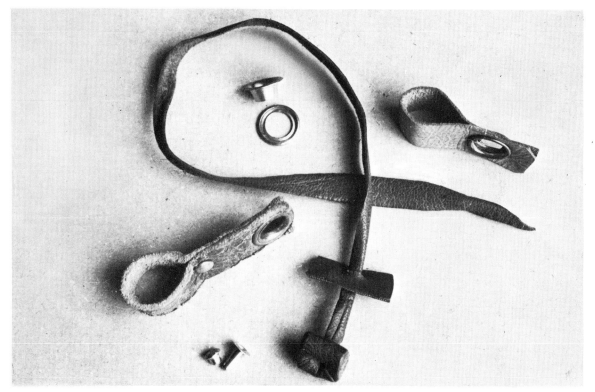

which your gloved hand can hold her. When you wish to let her go, you have only to let the free ends of the jesses slip through the eyelet, which they do with the greatest of ease. The hawk then does her flying with only a short stiff tab sticking straight out behind the lower part of her leg, not half such a hazard as the dangling jess with a slit in it, and far less trouble than changing jesses altogether.

There is an additional way of operating the Aylmeri. This is to change the jesses with the normal slit in them for a pair identical, but without the slit. These can be left on the whole time when the hawk is being flown. They eliminate the danger of the slit catching in something, yet keep the usefulness of having jesses with which to hold on to the hawk as soon as she is taken up after a flight.

A small square of rubber, say half an inch, with a hole in the middle, can be slid up the flying jess until

it comes against the eyelet: this prevents the flying jess from falling out of the eyelet when the bird is being flown, and getting lost.

The third form of jess is one invented by Mr. David Argue, excellent for sparrowhawks and merlins in particular, but not so suitable for other hawks. They should perhaps be called Argueri, on the same principle of naming as Aylmeri.

They consist of using a strong press stud to fasten the jess round each leg. Mr. Argue says that kestrels soon undo this press stud themselves, so it should obviously not be used for them. It is doubtful whether one should risk the holding of a larger bird than a sparrowhawk with this method. But it is certainly a handy way for jessing a bird with such long delicate legs as a sparrowhawk.

Whatever jesses or bells are chosen, a swivel is now essential. These can also be bought at the various places

A memorable Irish bag of magpies with the cast of peregrines (meaning two in number) responsible.

mentioned, but it is unwise to save trouble by buying a clip swivel, such as is used for dog leads. It is quite possible for the ends of the jesses to get under the clip itself and to come off, releasing the hawk inadvertently. You will then very likely lose the bird altogether.

It is probable that many hawks have been lost through just some episode as this, with equipment being unsuitable, worn out, or somehow avoidably defective. There are enough ways of losing a hawk by accidents which are entirely unpredictable and unavoidable, without employing a method which has been *known* to cause lost hawks. It is best therefore to use only the strongest sort of swivel. Hardy's, the fishing people, used to market a very good sized swivel for use in deepsea fishing, but this has now been discontinued, like so many useful things that for generations have been in small but steady demand.

The best chance of finding a swivel small, yet strong enough, is now in a yachting shop. Saddlers seem to be using more and more standard spring clip swivels: one

rarely finds an old-fashioned saddler's shop nowadays where all sorts of useful bits and pieces for hawking can be dug up.

Now comes the leash itself. It is no more than a stout piece of naturally greasy leather about two feet long, one end of which goes through the unoccupied eye of the swivel. The other end is tied to the perch or on whatever your hawk spends her non-flying time.

To prevent the leash slipping through the swivel loop, a knot or button must be made with the other end of the leash.

One of the pleasures of hawking is having nice looking, neat 'furniture' or equipment. Rather than just tying a knot in the end of the leash, it is more serviceable and much better looking to make a 'button' out of the end. There are various ways of doing this, and all are simple. Two or three folds, about an inch across, in the end of the leash, a hole punched with a large leather punch right through the folds and the other end of the leash passed through the holes and drawn tight, and the leash is ready. If the leather is tough, as

This picture of a Scottish haggard peregrine falcon
illustrates well the great power of the breast
and shoulders.

Most hawks like to perch as reasonably high as possible. A ground-level block or perch must often be irksome for an unhooded hawk, since it may be in a draughty or damp position. A high perch also gives her a little more exercise room, but it is advisable to have a good spring between five or six links of the chain to take up some of the jerk from the hawk's legs when she bates off hard from the perch. The chain is important since its weight acts as an effective decelerator.

This is an excellent example of haphazard falconry. The shortwing's bow perch has not been pushed fully into the ground, so that, as soon as the hawk bates, she will pull up the perch and drag it off. The jesses have not been greased or attended to for a long time to judge by the way they are twisted. At the swivel, the jess ends are not lying neatly one over the other, but one is at the bottom of the link where it interferes with the free play of the swivel. The bells are hanging down on loose bewits and the leash is so hard that it is standing up by itself. The hard button at the end is about to fall off and when this happens the hawk will escape, carrying jesses joined to the swivel dangling below her. But before this happens the falconer's knot will probably have come untied, since it has not been knotted correctly. To add to this catalogue of complaints, the ring round the perch is too small, probably causing it to jam, and making tying the leash difficult.

it should be, and the punch not sharp or big enough, cut a slit with a knife instead, one fold at a time.

Great care must be taken when cutting these slits not to go too near the sides of the leash. Otherwise when the slit comes under pressure by the leash being pulled through to tighten the knot, the whole button may begin to come apart. If this happens unnoticed, eventually the result will be a lost hawk due once more to faulty equipment.

The leash is very inclined to wear at the neck where it goes in to the swivel ring. This has been the cause of a lost hawk on many occasions in the past. But due to a simple invention by the American falconer, Thomas D. Ray of Colorado, this should never happen again.

Mr. Ray advocates slipping a small collar of nylon tube along the leash until it rests right against the button on the leash. The metal ring of the swivel then rests and works against this nylon, more than doubling the life of the leash. Mr. Ray also suggests putting a small nylon collar on the Aylmeri jesses where they bear upon the brass eyelet, another good idea.

Nylon tube of varying thickness can be bought at manufacturing chemists or hospital supply firms. A postcard to one or two names selected from the local *Yellow Pages* brought me an immediate offer of even the tiny amount wanted – perhaps a foot only of two or three different sizes, which would last for years. I have used the word nylon in a general layman's sense,

Above: this hawk likes a regular bath, provided it is a warm and sunny morning.

Left: the great breadth of shoulder of this two-year-old peregrine falcon is only really noticeable from this angle.

but the one offered was said to be polyvinyl tubing. There are many materials which will do the job well.

For a bird accustomed to perch or roost on trees, a perch needs to be provided whether at home during the night or out on the grass 'weathering', the term applied to hawks when sitting out during the daytime. These are the shortwings, where any sort of perch that can comfortably be gripped is suitable, perhaps a perch the length of the hawk's largest toe in diameter to enable her to grip comfortably. The most important point is that she should not be able to get tangled in the perch, eventually hanging upside down and dying, since such accidents invariably happen when there is no one about to rescue them. They must either be low to the ground, say 18 inches high or, if higher, must have a heavy screen of some sort stretched beneath to prevent the hawk, when she 'bates' or jumps off in fright or fury, from swinging underneath the perch and not being able to recover.

The longwinged falcon, the peregrines, lanners and others of the dark eyes and sickle-shaped wings, including the kestrel, are more at home during the day on a solid perch of round wood or stone, called a block. At night the longwing sits happily and safely on a screen perch (a long perch with a heavy piece of canvas or other non-fraying material slung underneath). The block must be designed so that the hawk cannot get tangled up round it. This happens more easily than one would suppose. The block may have a ring round the base of it, but the hawk might get this jammed.

Before you realize what has happened, she is flailing vainly at the ground, breaking feathers or, even worse, a leg, and perhaps throwing a fit in her panic.

To get round this difficulty, another small invention by the Scottish falconer, Walter Joynson, comes to the rescue. He advocates a round block of wood, circumference at the top about 23 inches and tapering to about 20 inches. The taper is important since it prevents the lower part of the block becoming filthy with droppings 'mutes' or 'slices' as they are called. Round the lower part of the block fasten a length of chain, not of course so light that there is danger of breaking it, yet

not so heavy as to be unyielding and angular. The chain needs, Mr. Joynson writes, to be loose enough, 'so that on pulling out of one link there is only an inch or so of freedom betwixt wood and chain, like,' he adds, 'a tight necklace on a girl's neck.'

On to the chain, with the chain passing freely through it, is fastened a ring, say one and a half inches in diameter, ideally a bullring, obtainable from any veterinary chemist. These rings have an arrangement whereby you can open them by slackening a small screw, close them over something, and then screw them tight.

In this case it is the chain. The hawk's leash is now fastened to the bullring. The whole contraption can now freely circle the block without the hawk getting stuck or hung up in any way.

I have tried this myself. It is an excellent improvement on the more traditional staple driven in to the top of the block, to which a swivel must be screwed before the hawk's leash can be tied on, or to the loose circle of heavy wire, with an eye twisted on it, which in theory turns freely round in a groove cut round the block half way down.

Both these latter methods are not free of the danger of entanglement, although they have been used satisfactorily by generations of falconers.

For the top of the block or perch, each falconer has his own preference. If a hawk is kept permanently on a soft-topped block or perch, she will not get corns or bruised feet, but on the other hand her nails will have nothing to prevent them growing unduly long and needle sharp. They will then need more frequent 'coping' or trimming, with clippers or file.

A longwing's block sometimes has a pad of concrete on top of the wood, or a piece of suitably shaped stone if some means of securing it to the wood can be found, or cork, or horsehide. This latter is particularly suitable for a shortwing's bow or ring perch.

Some people prefer to have the perch for the night time topped with canvas or carpet, and the daytime one of a harder substance, so that the hawk gets the best of both. But the nails will need watching whatever perches or blocks are used.

The almost legendary German falconer, Herr Renz Waller, pictured opposite in 1972, with his passage saker, Zarif, and setter, Prinz. Zarif is wearing a hood made by the finest of European hoodmakers, Karl Mullen, who died in 1936 at his home at the hawk-trapping centre at Valkenswaard, Holland.

The rebirth of falconry in Germany between the two world wars is almost entirely due to Herr Waller. It was he who interested Marshal Goering in the sport, and was responsible for setting up a State Falconry Mews and establishment in the grand manner. Goering became an enthusiastic supporter. In 1937, the sporting Marshal bought eight gyrfalcons from Iceland, which are not the pure white Greenland type, being more flecked with brown and reputed to be slower in flight than the Greenlanders. Whether they are slower or not must be very conjectural.

The Marshal also received three more Iceland gyrs that year as a present. Encouraged by this, and evidently spurred on by suggestions that Greenland gyrs were superior, he sent an expedition to Greenland in 1938. It returned triumphantly to the State Mews with six gyrfalcons. The Marshal declared at the time that his object was to re-introduce gyrfalcons into the German Alps where, he alleged, they had lived before the Glacial Age. He proposed to liberate them in conditions as near to their natural surroundings as possible. Unfortunately he had no success with this venture.

I am indebted for this information to the noted American falconer, ornithologist and scientist Col. William G. Mattox, left. It was Col. Mattox who led the last great expedition to Greenland in an endeavour to take a supply of gyrfalcons for purposes of falconry in 1951. The expedition was very successful, and they returned with no fewer than 11. Their success, however, was partially self-defeating, for the government later introduced a total ban on the export of gyrfalcons from Greenland, which is still in force at the time of writing. They are now protected during the nesting season, although occasional reports come through that the birds are shot at all times of the year.

Probably no one knows more about the Greenland gyrfalcon than Col. Mattox. He has conducted the most detailed research programme into many aspects of the bird's life which make fascinating reading. They are to be found in the scientific journal Polar Notes, number IX, May 1969. The picture shows Col. Mattox taking one of these most beautiful snow-white falcons out of the bow net before banding, weighing, measuring and releasing.

The picture on the left, shows another of the white birds with flecked back standing on the scales under the supervision of Col. R. A. Graham, Col. Mattox's assistant. The average weight of the 10 young falcons trapped was 3lb 3¼oz, while that of four young males was 2lb 7½oz.

The chances of anyone having an opportunity to man and fly a Greenland gyr are remote. No beginner, of course, would contemplate tackling one. They present even the experienced exponent with many problems, but few falconers can resist the occasional daydream of setting out one day with a Greenland falcon on his fist.

CHAPTER 6

A beginner who is really determined to get into falconry will never be deterred by the innumerable difficulties. The dabblers will soon be weeded out. It has never been an easy sport to take up, and is now more difficult than ever. To all the problems which never used to surround the sport to the same extent, the one of expense has now been added in all but the earliest stages.

A hawking 'establishment' will, of course, always have been an expensive affair. Around the turn of this century, there were several people employing professional falconers, with special transports, all manner of equipment, pigeon lofts kept to provide training birds, and much other paraphernalia. Hawks were regularly obtained from Holland as well as throughout Britain and the whole annual cost would have been high by any standards.

Today, the majority of people owning and flying a hawk consists of individuals who fly their hawk whenever they can get the time away from their day to day work or activity. They are doing everything themselves, and getting a great deal of pleasure out of it. There are more of these throughout the country than there have been for very many years and the general standard is probably higher than it used to be.

This is partly due to the necessity for taking greater care of the bird than when a lost hawk could quite easily be replaced by another. It is also due to a more intensified approach to the whole subject, and to the fact that much scientific research has been carried on into all aspects of bird life.

Fortunately there are still one or two hawking establishments maintained in the grand manner. It is impossible to over-emphasize the importance to falconry in general of such establishments, since it is only by practical work on all levels that hawking with its long traditions in Britain can be kept healthy and alive. In the autumn of 1972 an advertisement appeared in a magazine inviting applications for the post of professional falconer: 'Salary by arrangement, four weeks holiday a year . . .' This is an excellent sign of the way hawking is being kept healthily alive in Britain today. There was no lack of replies to the advertisement.

Vicomte Adolphe de Spoelberch from Belgium, left,
is one of a growing number of visitors from abroad
who are taking an increasing interest in the sporting
activities of Britain. The Vicomte has a property
in Glencoe, Scotland and is seen here hawking
with M. Jean-Pierre Bordes, right, from Toulouse.

The lad with his kestrel contributes just as much. The important thing is to keep alive the whole chain of activities, from this same kestrel being flown hesitantly at mice in a farmyard, to the falcon from a cadge of half a dozen peregrines stooping at 100 miles an hour on a grouse moor. Between these two lies a great range of hawking activity. These pages are designed, as has already been said, to contribute to the maintenance of this range of activities.

It is sometimes urged that the fewer enthusiasts who come into the sport, the more chance it will have of survival because there are already not enough hawks to go round. But it is readily proved that there are enough hawks to go round, it is only that they are not the same sort of hawks that used to be available. Apart from the kestrel, the home bred hawk can hardly be looked to for hawking. The birds must come from abroad, under properly controlled conditions.

This makes everything more difficult and more expensive for the learner to start, which is the reason he needs all the encouragement he can get. Criticisms that people should not be encouraged if they have not the determination to get on with it by themselves are not valid. As said before, without the present increase in interest, the hawking fraternity would become such a tiny voice in the national babel of sectional interests that elimination would very soon overtake it. Fortunately there are signs that owing to more and more individuals being determined to take a practical interest in many parts of the country, the voice of falconry will not be so easily stifled.

There are now groups in England, Scotland and Wales of people meeting together to discuss their hawks and to fly them at whatever suitable quarry can be found. This is a most healthy sign.

In France, Germany, Austria, the Netherlands, even Switzerland, in Spain, Belgium and Australia, interest is reviving, in some cases after decades of neglect. In the United States, there is intense interest among what will always be a very limited band of enthusiasts, as in other countries. This all means that throughout the world there is one group of people more closely concerned with the fostering and preservation of birds of prey than has ever existed, and at a time when birds of prey are suffering most from man's creeping eliminations of the wild.

In some parts of Europe, goshawks and other hawks suitable for falconry are destroyed by the hundreds, and in some cases by the thousand – unbelievable numbers, but nevertheless largely verifiable. Every hawk that can be saved from this truly appalling destruction by a falconer, either in the same country or abroad, is one more rescued. The more falconers there are, the more chance there may be of reducing the numbers of hawks deliberately destroyed throughout the world.

An awareness of the possibilities of falconry in the modern world has largely been built up in Britain over the past dozen years or so by the great public spectacle of a flying display put on by the British Falconers' Club at the now annual Game Fair, which is held in a different part of the country each time. For thousands of people this is the first time they have ever seen hawks and falcons at close quarters, and certainly the first time they have ever seen them flying, stooping to the lure at high speeds over the crowd, or merely sitting out on their blocks and perches in the 'weathering ground' throughout the duration of the Fair.

These displays have undoubtedly done more than anything else to arouse a new generation of interest and are responsible for the increasingly healthy collective and sympathetic attitude being adopted towards the hawks themselves and to their training and flying.

The action of the Club in staging these demonstrations, and in maintaining a tent at Fairs where experienced falconers can answer questions from anyone interested in the sport, has been criticized on the score of creating undue interest and putting too much pressure on the already strained resources of the hawking world.

This argument has been referred to before. It can only be a matter of opinion whether it is the right or the wrong thing to do. But the British Falconers

One is never too young to get a hawking team together. Although the pointer is not an integral part of a sparrowhawk outing, Wond, Adam and the sparrowhawk, Star, seem ready to give it a try.

A peregrine on a screen perch, drawn by Otto Kals.

Otto Kals.

Club, with nearly 500 members, represents the hard core of practising falconers throughout Britain. Its hand is greatly strengthened in the defence of falconry by welcoming to its ranks anyone who genuinely wishes to fly a hawk for himself.

There are now other organizations holding public flying displays throughout the country at shows and fairs, and a widely representative Falconry Centre in Gloucestershire where one of Europe's foremost falconers, Mr. Phillip Glasier, maintains an establishment of the greatest interest, referred to in more detail in the section on breeding hawks in captivity on page 146 and the appendix.

Let us now see what is to be done with the hawk which the beginner has finally obtained: it is either a young bird taken from the nest just before it would have left it on its own account, or a bird acquired by some other means, perhaps from abroad.

The very first requirement is to calm the bird; to dismiss from its mind all the uproar, noise, movement and distress experienced if the bird has come by plane or travelled any distance, and to only a slightly lesser degree if it has been snatched from a nest, scooped off a branch, or trapped in some device terrifying to a highly sensitive bird like a hawk.

This is done by gentleness of voice, quietness of movement and dim light. Patience, encouragement, smooth moving about, all are essential if the hawk is to allow herself to enter into a relationship with her new partner in life. It is, however, a partnership which rests largely on food and the correct provision of it by the dominant partner.

The hawk must be made to accept food freely. Nothing can be achieved until she is eating healthily. Before bringing her home, a room or some sort of large hut must have been prepared which can be made completely dark, yet with an arrangement for progressively letting light in.

This is not complicated and any room will do. The greatest essential is for it to be dry and draught free. Nothing makes a hawk ill more quickly – or indeed, most birds or animals – than having to stand in a damp draught. One tends to forget that although the bird

in the wild may spend all night in drizzling rain and sharp wind, she has chosen her own position with the best available shelter. If she finds herself uncomfortable she is free to move either a little or a lot, or go somewhere quite different. When tied to a perch or block, she has no option: it may well not be a place she would choose on her own account.

It is therefore all the more important to make her perches as free from such discomforts as possible.

The first perch, which must be ready to receive her, will need to be a screen perch. This is a simple piece of wood, either a natural, not too rough, long branch free of all knots, twigs or other projections, including rough bark, with some heavy material hanging below. The object of this is quite straightforward. If the perch had no canvas or other heavy screen hanging below and the bird, when secured to the perch, tried to fly off in fear or anger, she might as soon as she reached the extent of her fastenings, her jesses, swing back with a jolt to a position upside down under the perch.

From this she might easily not be able to clamber back on to the perch, even with flailing wings. This must therefore never be forgotten, even with well-mannered and fully trained birds. Do not let experience have to teach you that the screen really is necessary by finding your hawk one morning hanging upside down, dead from suffocation. Also ensure that the screen is not made of coarse meshed sacks. Your hawk can catch her claws in this as she returns to the perch and may be unable to disengage them.

A useful idea is to make the screen of a length of canvas hanging down about three feet, and nailed securely along the underside of the perch in the middle. A few pieces of wood or something else a bit weighty can be laid in the fold to keep the sides taut. When the bird needs to kick against the screen to recover her perch, the screen remains reasonably taut and greatly helps her up.

For the hawk actually to stand on, a thick piece of carpet, the underside uppermost, makes a good grip, but must be renewed when it begins to get dirty from food. The carpet needs firmly tacking along

Colonel Carnie, the American falconer, below with his gyrfalcon and opposite with his particularly large female passage goshawk.

the underneath, and at the two ends over the perch to prevent it fraying. Shoulder height from the ground is a good enough measurement. Hawks hate being towered over, especially when in the early stages of training.

Before you collect your bird, the simple arrangements for securing her must be prepared. You can buy all these at one of the addresses given at the end of the book, but if it is your very first effort, then you are strongly recommended to make them all yourself – with the exception of the metal swivel and the bells. These have been described and illustrated earlier and, I hope, leave no doubt as to how it should be done.

Aylmeri jesses, already described, are much to be encouraged. Two sets are needed, one for daily use when tied to the perch or block, the other, with no slit in the end, for use when flying.

All this equipment will be ready in your darkened 'mews', a word now used for any place where hawks are kept, but originally only where they moulted or 'mewed'. Carry her into the mews still in the box or basket. If you have had to travel a long distance to get her, do not attempt to do anything with her at the airport, apart from making sure she is still alive. It will not be much help if she has expired on the journey, but at least you might try to claim something from the airline who may have treated her unduly roughly. This would probably be difficult to prove, and anyway it will be found that cases of bad handling by an airline are very infrequent. They normally take a lot of trouble provided the box or crate has been properly and clearly marked 'Live Bird'.

You will have done what you could to see that no wire netting has been used in the box. If the hawk gets up against this, as she probably would, she can scrape the front of her head or beak badly on the wire. Also, if clinging to the wire with her feet, her wings and tail feathers can be destroyed, which will be a disaster.

You will also hope that her tail may have been protected for the journey by having bands of sticky paper bound round the feathers, which can save them much damage. It is a useful tip to know if sending

any hawk yourself on a journey.

Once in your mews, shut the door behind you and lock it on the inside if you can. This prevents someone bursting in at a crucial moment with an offer of help, terrifying the hawk which you are at such pains to calm, and perhaps even resulting in its immediate loss as it streaks out to daylight through the door. This is not an unknown occurrence.

A dim light is a great help, even a necessity if it is the very first hawk you have handled, and the hawk has herself never been manned or partially trained. A candle in a far corner of the room is excellent, giving a soft light, not enough to enable the bird to make out disquieting details, nor natural enough for her to think that it is perhaps daylight towards which she must try to escape.

At this stage, you will not need a glove to protect your hand if the bird is a kestrel or something similar. If you have acquired something more formidable, wear a glove, not so thick as to make moving your hand difficult. This is not your regular hawking glove yet. It is a good idea to have one made to the pattern of your left hand – Eastern falconers use the right hand, and there is no point in not conforming to this old tradition if you are righthanded. If you are left-handed, then of course you will find it easier to hold the hawk the other way round.

Open the box very slowly and carefully without jerks or noise apart from soothing words. You want the hawk to get used to you as soon as possible and she will respond to your voice more quickly than to anything else. Speak softly to her the whole time.

She is unlikely to move to begin with, and you will see her form squatting on the bottom of the box. Put both hands down smoothly and firmly directly on to her back, with fingers over each shoulder containing the wings and thumbs meeting together in the middle of her back, her head facing forward. Lift her straight up as smoothly and steadily as you can and put her feet against the side of the perch. She will grip the carpet of the perch at once, at least feeling something solid. At that instant take your hands off her and she will clamber on to the perch, using her wings to help

keep her steady and maintain her balance.

If by bad luck the bottom of the box has had sacking or some soft material on it, and not canvas, she will probably be dug into it. This is a complication and you will probably need an assistant to take her out if there is not to be an unseemly and frightening episode right at the beginning of her life with you, something you want particularly to avoid.

Carry on in the same way as before, in this event, lifting her to the extent of her legs, and get the assistant very gently to disengage her claws from the sacking or whatever was holding her to the box. Smooth movements and gentle talk the whole time are essential.

If when you open the box softly she is found to be on her back striking and screaming, quietly close the box up again. Put on your new thick hawking glove, re-open the box very slowly and let her grab your glove as savagely as she likes. When she has got a good hold, raise your glove up and lay it along the middle of the perch as gently as you can without damaging any feathers. You may need to set her upright with the other hand.

But as soon as she feels a firm perch beneath her, she will tend to grip that in preference to your hand and you can then gently withdraw your glove along the perch until you are free of her and she is standing up on her perch.

If at first she declines to use her legs at all, perhaps through cramp or fear, keep her balanced on top of the perch by steadying her with both hands if necessary, and she will soon recover the use of her legs.

This is all being done in the very dim light of your candle. Keep matches in your pocket in case the withdrawal from the box has not gone smoothly and the candle has been blown out by angry wing beats.

You must now put on her jesses. If you have practised enough, or have acquired the knack already, you may prefer to slip your hands into the box before you take her out of it and put the jesses on while she is still in the box.

But if it is your first bird, you will prefer to have a bit more room in which to operate.

The eight pictures below and opposite give a step-by-step guide to a falconer's knot for tying a hawk's leash to the ring on a perch or block. This is done with only one hand, the hawk being on the other hand. The method will, of course, be reversed for left-handed falconers, who will carry their hawks on the right hand, leaving the left hand free to do the work.

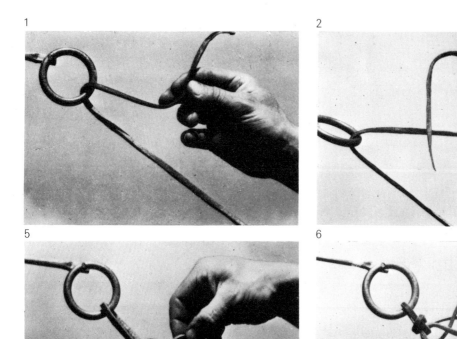

1

2

5

6

It is essential anyway to have practised on a piece of wood, or any substitute for the hawk's leg, before trying to put jesses on a new hawk for the first time. It would be advisable to put traditional jesses on to begin with, changing to Aylmeri when you have both got used to each other, perhaps after a week or so. It is useful to have a stuffed bird to practise on: it is possible to pick one up for a few shillings if you search long enough.

Talking gently all the time, fasten your jesses, slip each end through the same loop of the swivel, but going through that loop one way with one jess, and then the opposite way with the other jess, so that the tips of the jess lie neatly on either side of the jess when pulled over the whole swivel.

If you have a spring clip already tied to the middle

of the screen perch in the centre of your piece of carpet, it is easy to clip the free loop of the swivel on to this, and your hawk is secure.

Otherwise, merely slip the leash through the free loop of the swivel, tie a single knot to prevent it sliding along the leash, and then tie the leash to the middle of the carpeting with the simple knot illustrated above. Then slip the loose ends down between the two folds of your screen well out of the way. Every publication on hawking refers to the falconer's knot. There is no mystery about this.

It is merely the simplest and most efficient knot for securing a leash to a perch or block, the point about it being that it can be tied very swiftly with one hand only, and equally quickly untied, since the other hand is occupied by holding the hawk.

3

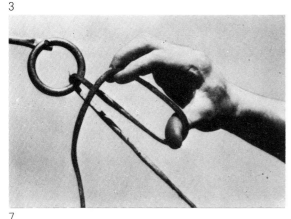

4

7

8

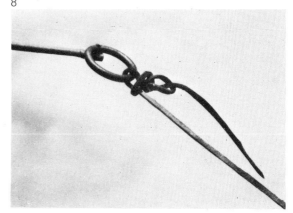

Practise it thoroughly, together with the other details of jessing and belling, before your hawk arrives and you will be thankful that you have done so. Make the knot second nature to you, and tie it double so that you never have cause to lose your hawk through a carelessly tied knot as illustrated on page 71.

The traditional way to gain the confidence of a new hawk and to start her on the vital stage of being properly manned, or tamed without seeming to relinquish any of her spirit of proud independence, is to 'wake' her. This consists of sitting up with her uninterruptedly for a whole night and perhaps another day and night, so that she gets no rest (nor, of course, does the falconer). Finally she reaches, one hopes, the opinion that she and her new joint friend have been through an ordeal together, which warrants

her placing some confidence in him, and through sheer hunger she is obliged to accept some food from him.

Once she has accepted food, the whole process has really started.

It is not necessary to go to the great lengths of a full-scale 'wake', but many people find it the most satisfying, and brings the quickest and most enduring results. But it is extremely exhausting, and unless carefully arranged at a weekend, or at some free period, many people just cannot spend the time on it.

The really important thing is that she should accept her food from the falconer himself and not be left to have her first feed on her own, with a bit of meat or bird strapped to her perch to take when she finally feels like eating it.

Top right: a pair of home bred red-tailed hawks.

Top far right: a passage saker.

Below right: a seven-year-old tundra falcon.

Below far right: a male eyass tiercel gyr, known as a jerkin.

All her food should come only from the falconer, her partner, on all occasions during the initial manning and training. This is the chief way the bond can be forged between the two. It is best to stay with her on her arrival at least until she has accepted some food, however little an amount. She must not on any account be allowed to feed by herself at this stage if the whole process is not to be greatly and unnecessarily drawn out. There will be exceptions to this, depending on whether the newly arrived hawk has been given a large feed just before its journey, which would not be advisable, and whether the bird is of a species which can go long periods without food.

Some birds, particularly a merlin, will feed almost at once, and the whole process to flying free can take as little as five or six days. For a peregrine, this can take under a fortnight with skilled work, whereas a goshawk may take up to a month. Most beginners may find these periods considerably longer, but it can be done in these times, and even shorter periods are frequently taken by experienced falconers.

Other types of hawk will vary in the time needed to train and enter them. But so much depends on the character and temperament of the bird (and of the falconer, too), on the climate, the time of year, food available, and general conditions, that it is pointless to state how long the training should take. Some people are able to devote days of uninterrupted attention to a new hawk. Others cannot get the time to do this. The results will, of course, vary greatly under these conditions, but it is only natural that the more concentrated time that can be spent on a new hawk, the sooner the hawk will be ready to fly free.

As the new hawk first begins to pick at tantalising food drawn across her toes while she stands in the dim light of the mews, there is a feeling of great excitement for the new falconer. This is the very first successful step. The hawk has responded to his own personal effort, and the bond is beginning to be forged, the bond which will finally be put to the test when the hawk is first cast off to fly free – and to come back to the falconer, or not, according to how he has carried out the training.

Mr. Croft Slater's haggard tiercel (wild caught, adult male) red-naped shahin, pronounced shah-heen. Tame and attractive longwing desert falcons, the various shahins are very desirable hawks but they are more delicate in my experience and far more difficult to keep in good health than the peregrine. They seldom achieve the brilliance of a good peregrine and, although they are easier to get results from, they seldom give of their best unless exactly cared for.

She can be left after she has taken her first feed. Thin strips of fresh beef are appreciated by most hawks. For her very first feed, it is a good idea to let her eat as much as she will take. This will restore her digestion to full activity, provided the strips are very thin, and give her a chance of restoring all her shattered systems, both nervous, mental and physical, to normal operation.

Lumps of beef may easily make her sick and should anyway never be given to a hawk in sizes that she can just swallow whole. They must either be small enough to be absorbed readily, or big enough to require her to tear shreds off them herself.

The next day, according to how quietly she is settling down, a little daylight can be let into the mews, just enough to see by, but again not so much for her to see clearly and be alarmed. If she gets a real fright by suddenly being confronted by the moon face of the falconer close up to her, all the good of having got her to accept food may be cast away. The falconer then has to start all over again to regain her confidence.

This will be a setback and is much to be avoided.

In India and the East the practice of 'seeling' is still followed, a very efficient and harmless way of gradually restoring full daylight to a newly captured or taken hawk. It entails passing a thread through the bottom lid of each eye and tying the threads together on top of the head after drawing the two lids up to close them. This is a great deal easier to do than one would think, and never appears to worry the hawk in the slightest. Instead of tying a knot, the ends can be held together by wax. To slacken them progressively, it is only necessary in this case to pull the ends very gently.

Each time a little more light is needed, the thread knot is slackened a little bit, allowing the eye to open more and more, until the thread can finally be completely discarded and the hawk's eyes returned to normal.

For some reason, this practice is frowned on in Britain and now not used at all. It has only rarely been practised in Europe.

Anyone who carries a menacing harpy eagle is
lucky to lose only part of his thumb, as has just
happened to this Austrian falconer. No beginner
should be tempted to acquire a bird like this — its
undoubtedly magnificent appearance is no
compensation for the unending nightmare of
looking after it.

CHAPTER 7

There are some simple ways of retaking your hawk
which has gone off on its own, either through broken
and ill-maintained jesses, leash or swivel, or her darting
suddenly out of hand before being properly tied to
the perch or secured in the glove, or declining to
return when being flown free.

The methods themselves are easy enough to
arrange. Whether the hawk will co-operate by appear-
ing in the right place at a suitable time to be approached
is quite another matter. There is nothing new in any
of these ways, but they have all been tried and found
to work. Many falconers invent other methods of
their own which may be just as effective.

1. A bow net, perhaps the simplest of all. Get a
piece of nylon or string netting, old herring net, or
any light netting of about one inch diameter mesh.
Cut out an oval shape about four feet across, or if it
is a square and you do not wish to cut it, leave it as a
square. Make a light metal rod about three feet long
into a half-hoop, with an eye at each end: heavy
fencing wire is ideal. Take this to where you think
the hawk may come. Lay the net flat on the ground
and stake one edge to the ground with wire pegs or
pieces of stick. Tie the opposite edge to the hooped
rod, and fold it back on to the staked-down edge,
having secured the two eyed ends of the rod to the
ground with a couple of pieces of strong fencing wire
bent at one end into a hook to go through the eye
on the end of the hooped rod.

Stake down a particularly enticing piece of food
on a line roughly between the two eyes of the rod.
Fasten a long fishing line or length of garden twine,
or indeed, any thin strong cord to the rod, not directly
in the middle since this would catch on the staked-
down food, but a bit to the side. One each side is a
good idea, with a fencing-wire eyed stake to pass
both through.

It is obvious enough how to work it. When the
hawk comes to feed, a quick pull on the cord from a
hiding place perhaps 100 yards away covers the hawk
with the net, and she is caught. Go up at once and
carefully extricate her, using every care not to break
a feather and, if necessary, cutting the net away with

This lanneret, given to Robin Haigh by David Rooke, was finally lost flying at rooks.

scissors if she is hopelessly tangled. It should always be possible to do this without having to cut the net so that the contraption can be kept permanently available for emergencies.

In former days, a live pullet or pigeon or some such lure was tied to the ground, which made an infallible bait for a lost or wild hawk once it was found. But nowadays, of course, a live bait or lure is never used in Britain. A small refinement to the bait is a dead bird, staked to the ground as mentioned, but with another piece of fishing line or nylon tied to one of its wings. When the hawk appears, a tweaking of this line makes the wing flap in a very realistic way which few hawks can resist. It is the wing which catches the eye quicker than anything else. Likewise it is the flicker of a hawk's wing on the falconer's fist which is instantly detected by birds from quite a distance, far more than the normal moving about of bird or falconer.

This bow net is particularly useful when you have found the kill which your escaped or wild hawk has made, and although she has started to feed on it, she will not stay when you approach, but flies off. Set the bow net round the kill itself, staking the kill down instead of a new bait, and you will catch her when she returns to her kill and you are out of sight.

The only disadvantage of this good trap is that the operator has to sit beside it all the time in order to operate it at the crucial moment. In *Falconry For You,* an automatic adaptation is described using some pieces of catapult elastic. But if this is used it is still necessary to visit the trap very often, since a hawk taken in it may do herself a great deal of physical damage, if left any length of time. The shock, rage and fear which she will be occasioned can be almost more harmful. It is bad enough when she is released as soon as caught, but if she has to wait any time in such turmoil she may take a very long time to recover, and will perhaps hold it against the falconer for the rest of her life. Hawks have very strong feelings, and the falconer should always respect these on all occasions. She may never forgive a loss of temper, angry shouts or petulant movements.

Even if she does forgive them, it is one more hurdle to be taken in gaining her respect and confidence, without which no falconer can have a satisfactory relationship with his hawk.

It is the delicacy of this relationship which is one of the great attractions of forming a partnership with a hawk. Every possible care must be taken not to rupture this fine balance.

2. A large length of fine mesh nylon, say six or eight yards long, strung on three small bamboos or long light branches stuck in the ground, with bait in the middle, is perhaps the simplest of all. This and other nets depend for their best success on the use of live birds as the bait, which can of course be rescued as soon as the hawk has tangled itself into the net. But it may not be legal in Britain, so is not used by the modern falconer in this country. Elsewhere, the practice continues, and escaped hawks are soon retaken if they are still in the vicinity.

The net is draped loosely enough, and the branches or bamboos are flimsy enough, for the whole thing to collapse as soon as touched by the flying hawk. Again she must be rescued as soon as possible.

3. For catching a hawk which is not so wild as to disappear altogether, but yet will not come down from a tree, or insists on flying round and ignoring all usual lures, a system of snares can be very effective. I always carry this little piece of equipment in my bag if flying an unreliable hawk, and have on one occasion taken a wild hawk with it. It is a small canvas jacket with as many nylon nooses as there is room for, fastened all over it. It is simplicity itself. In former days used round a live lure, but, as mentioned before, not nowadays in Britain, it is tied round the body of a dead pigeon, pullet, rabbit, or whatever is most likely to appeal to the hawk which it is intended to capture.

A fishing line is the best to operate it. An extra long line, over 100 yards contained on a spinning reel, or ordinary fishing reel, can easily be kept in the falconer's bag. When jerked along from 100 yards away, twitching and bumping with wings at all angles, the effect is nearly as good as with a live bait.

A longwing finds this very exciting and a goshawk

in a wood may find it well-nigh irresistible.

4. A method not so popular nowadays, called 'winding up', involves walking round and round an errant hawk which comes to a feed, but will not allow herself to be taken up, with a long light line pegged say 30 yards from the grounded hawk at one end, and paid out as the falconer walks round in a wide circle. This way the hawk's legs may soon be wound together with the constantly circling cord. But this is difficult to do if the ground is not particularly free of tufts or nettle stems, thistles, or bits of stiff grass. It also requires an arrangement of sloping-in feathers or smooth slivers of wood round the place where it is expected the hawk will stand, in order to slide the winding line up above the hawk's feet.

This was also used as with the bow net, for taking up a hawk after it had been *flown at hack*. Flying at hack is a system whereby an eyass is taken from the nest and partially manned and trained, and then turned loose for perhaps a month to develop natural powers of flight. These cannot be so well developed if it is kept permanently on a block and only flown round for exercise at the lure during training. It is a risky process these days, unless the falconer can be in good open country – or indeed, anywhere – where the loose bird, flying about at random all day long, will not be shot or trapped. The hawk is fed every day on the board of food, known as the hack-board, and comes morning and evening to get his food. But as his strength builds up and he gets more confidence, he will begin to think about killing for himself. Up to this time he is entirely reliant on the hack-board for his food.

After perhaps three weeks or so, varying according to the initial condition of the hawk and to his general surroundings, he will kill and perhaps not come back to the hack-board that day. If he is lucky he may kill again the next day, and again not return to the hack-board.

He will now have to be caught up at the very first time he does return to the hack-board, otherwise he has hacked himself back to the wild and is lost to the falconer altogether, with small chance of recovery.

It is a very exciting experience hacking a hawk in this way. He must get the most benefit possible from his period of freedom, but how long to leave him out? If the falconer begins to lose his nerve and think the precious eyass is never going to return, he takes him up, with the bow net round the hack-board, long before, perhaps, he need do so. On the other hand, over-confidence allows him to leave the eyass out too long, and he never returns.

There are very great benefits to be had from this process, which is normally only applied to a young peregrine. He can become a far better flyer if well hacked than if he has never had this great experience. But if the hawk is the falconer's only bird, the falconer may suffer sleepless nights wondering whether he has left the hawk out too long at hack. Why did he not come back at all today? There was no sign of a kill anywhere about. Has anyone been setting traps which he might have got into? Was that a shot I heard earlier in the day? Why did I not take him up yesterday when he came confidently to the hack-board?

Worse still, and not a modern development, has someone come secretly, set a bow net with an enticing bait, trapped and stolen the precious bird?

It is not surprising that few people feel brave enough to hack a hawk, or have enough hawks to be able to risk any at hack.

95

CHAPTER 8

It is important to arrange matters so that you can spend as much time as possible, during the vital first three days of the new hawk's arrival, alone with her. Concentration of effort during this period will be well repaid in the hawk coming to hand far more quickly than if only an hour or two a day can be spared.

She has been kept in the darkened mews with more and more light being added until she feeds without fear from the falconer's hand, standing on her perch with the minimum of 'bating', as wild efforts to fly off are called.

It is helpful to get her to stand on your gloved fist when she eats, pulling at the piece of beef, pigeon, starling, rabbit, chicken or whatever you can get to feed her with, which you are holding tightly in the glove. To get her to stand on the glove, put the gloved hand behind her and gently press against the back of her legs. To save herself over-balancing she will step backwards up on to the glove. Likewise if she will not get off the glove when she has finished feeding, hold her slowly forward and rest the underneath of her tail on top of the perch, lowering your hand very gradually, being careful not to pull her off backwards when the jesses are fully extended from the swivel, but just pressing the underneath of her tail down on to the perch by the action of lowering the whole bird an inch or two.

This will have the same effect as the manoeuvre to get her on to the glove to begin with. She will step backwards up on to the perch.

When you can approach her in broad daylight on her perch without her showing undue apprehension, the traditional jesses can be replaced by the Aylmeri jesses which it is hoped you will consider worthwhile.

Do not attempt this until she is very tame, since the operation entails a certain amount of fiddling about round the legs. If she gets upset at this stage, it will be a check to her progress and time will have been lost in having to go over the same ground again to restore the lost confidence.

The Aylmeri need a rivet each close to the leg, to enclose the jess tightly enough for the whole foot not to be able to pass through and the bird thus escape, nor

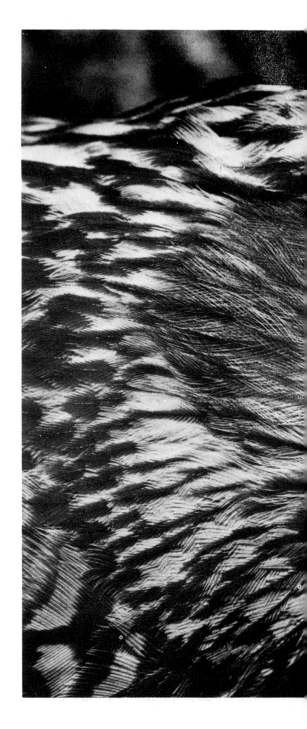

This fine example of a working goshawk belongs
to Mr. George Mussared.

soon breaks, with the same result.

Similarly with the eyelet for the jess. Special pliers
are again available for closing the surround to the
eyelet, but in this case they are hardly necessary, since
any ordinary pliers can be used to bend back the soft
brass rim. This has to be done bit by bit in order to
keep the rim even. The special pliers, of course, would
make an even job, with maximum turn over of the
rim in one movement. The lower jaw is a sort of
shallow cup, and the upper jaw flat, or with a slightly
raised round projection over which the eyelet is held
centrally in place.

In former days, falconers used always to attach
small name discs or labels to the jesses, called varvells.
This went out of use for some reason, but it is a wise
precaution to take. It is well worth having your name
and telephone number engraved on a very small label
of aluminium or any suitable material, and rivet this
on to the tab of the Aylmeri, not, of course to the
jesses themselves.

Complete one leg and secure its jess to the swivel,
and then to the perch, before starting on the other. If
the hawk is beginning to get upset in the middle of
the operation, do not plunge on to get the job finished
at all costs, but leave her until she is thoroughly settled
before trying the next leg. This is the reason for
completely securing one leg at a time to the perch.

It is also important not to have her standing un-
secured at any time. Experience has shown that this is
always the moment when some sudden and entirely
unexpected loud noise occurs, frightening the hawk
into attempted flight. If she does not achieve the worst
result by escaping from a suddenly open door, at least
she may fly desperately round the mews room clinging
to anything she can get a foothold on. She then has to
be recaptured in a flurry of disarranged and perhaps
broken feathers and, worse than the feathers, a greatly
disturbed attitude of mind.

If she does get loose at an early stage in the mews,
keep very still, talking to her all the time in a soothing
voice until she does perch on something. Gradually
darken the room again if this can be done from inside,
which is desirable. Or go quietly outside if it has to be

so tightly that it grips the leg without moving freely
round it. This will not be uncomfortable for the hawk
but might easily be responsible for dislocating her
thigh if she bates off against the perch, or even from
your hand when carrying her. Enough room must
also be left for the leather to swell very slightly if it
gets wet. For safety two rivets are needed, in addition
to the large eyelet through which the jess is going to
pass.

A special tool for clamping rivets neatly and quickly
can be bought. It is worth having; it is only a form of
pliers with a projection on one jaw which allows the
rivet to be splayed out on the underside of the leather.
There are various forms of rivet obtainable, and the
falconer must please himself over which he thinks is
best. It should not be so small that it may easily pull
through the leather, allowing the two folds of the
Aylmeri to come apart at the leg and the bird's foot to
slip easily through, releasing her. Nor does it need to
take up so much of the width of the leather that the
small amount of leather on either side of the rivet

The Cooper's hawk, a North American bird, can be very fierce and is ready to tackle almost anything, including, sometimes, his partner. The three in the picture are, from left to right, Trouble, a western female eyass whose flying weight is $11\frac{1}{2}$oz, Coopa, an eastern intermewed female passager, $15\frac{1}{2}$oz (intermewed means a hawk which has had at least one moult in captivity; passager is a hawk caught wild before its first moult), and Fred, an eastern tiercel eyass, flying at 9oz.

Bokhara, a golden eagle, belongs to ornithologist and falconer, Mr. Philip Wayre.

done that way, leaving just enough light to see her. Go slowly and quietly up to her, speaking to her all the time, and get her to step backwards on to the glove. She can then be carried gently to the centre of her perch and the jessing operation completed or, if she is still upset, postponed until later. Remember to lock the door so that no one goes in by mistake. When you yourself enter into a mews where there is a loose hawk, remember to go in shutting the door very quietly and quickly behind you. A hawk has an amazing facility for streaking out the instant daylight appears through an opened door.

The next stage is for your hawk to make a positive move towards you to take her food. This goes for whatever sort of hawk it is. It can be done to begin with by holding the food just out of reach, so that she has to bend forward. She is up to this stage still secured to the swivel and leash, remaining tied to the perch.

But soon, depending how much time the falconer is able or prepared to spend with her, she must be released from bondage to the perch and allowed, or at least encouraged, to take a step off her perch on to the glove. As time goes on she will make a bigger and bigger step, finally needing a large wing-assisted jump to reach the glove. The leash this time has been untied and made free of the perch, but firmly held in the unoccupied right hand.

From here, the distance is made greater every time. A further stage is the fastening of a long line, perhaps heavy garden twine, or a thick fishing line, to the loop of the swivel which does not contain the jess ends and the taking off of the leash altogether – all being done quietly and gently while the hawk stays on her perch. The falconer stands a few yards away, holding the long line, or 'creance' as it is known, and calls her to his fist in which he holds her feed, with the whistle he is going to use in future to summon her, or special cry or sound of his own.

If there is not room in the mews or hawk house to perform this operation, she must be transferred to her outside perch or block. The shortwings prefer a perch, which approximates to the tree branch in which they normally perch or 'take stand'. The longwing more normally stands on a ledge or stone if given the choice, and is therefore better accommodated always on a block, as the small round perch is called. This suits the longwing foot better than that of the shortwing.

Outside perches can be of a large variety. For the longwing a simple wooden perch with a variety of tops is quite adequate – even without the refinement of different tops. Leather can be tacked on top, or a concrete surface made by sinking a hole in the wood and making a sort of concrete plug which rests there by its own weight and is steady for the hawk to stand on. The concrete is not as good as stone, but serves to keep the hawk's nails from getting too long and sharp. A stone top is, of course, far more difficult to arrange. It is doubtful whether it is worth preparing anything other than a plain wooden perch for a longwing, until you have had time to have an opinion of your own as to what is best.

The object of these pages is simply to get the beginner started. To go into all the pros and cons of every different type of perch, and indeed all the equipment or hawk 'furniture', would take a chapter on its own. The same applies to the birds themselves and to all the different methods of training them, and the different quarry at which they can be made to fly.

I am not attempting here to lay down the law on every single matter, nor to discuss the dozens of different sorts of flight to be had in the hawking world. There are other books devoted to all these individual aspects.

The beginner must get started in a sound and general way before he can progress to personal variation on traditional themes, and would be well advised not to try any fancy work until he has acquired a proper grounding.

This is one of the reasons why one cannot stress too strongly the advisability of getting a home bred kestrel to start with, and not embarking on a more exotic or demanding hawk which may, the way things are at the moment, be more easily obtained.

Perches for the shortwing can also be very simple, and need only to be so. The same argument about a perch applies here as it does for the longwing. Make

My female passage goshawk, Minerva, below, halfway through her 13th moult in 1972. She has over 100 brown hares to her credit and much other quarry. It is as a result of a battle with a 10lb hare that her right wing is now held 'at the droop' as seen in the picture opposite of her nearing completion of her moult. Minerva came as a passager from Swedish Lapland through the good offices of Colonel Lindquist of Malmö, and usually flies at 2lb 13oz or 14oz.

the simplest one to start with, and gradually make up your own mind which you think is best. This is a branch bent to form a bow, say three feet long, with a stout wire betwen the two ends, and a ring on the wire to tie the leash to. The ring for these shortwing perches, as well as for the longwing, can be the one which is sold in agricultural supply shops as a bullring, already mentioned: the biggest size for a goshawk, and the middle size for every other. These rings have the advantage of being hinged, so that they can be put round a stake or wire after the rest of the work is done. They are then screwed together again with a very small screw provided.

The leash is tied to the ring with the falconer's knot as shown in the pictures on pages 86 and 87.

Both these perches are only one or two feet above the ground, so that the hawk sits very low. When

setting her on the perch, or taking her up, or indeed, doing anything with her, it is necessary to kneel, so as not to tower over her.

Another point is not to stare directly into the hawk's face if she fixes her gaze upon you. There is no doubt that she can be distinctly upset and made ill at ease if you do not look away as soon as she starts her stare at you.

With the shortwing, such as a goshawk, the final object will be to release her from your gloved fist at her quarry which may be almost anything to be found normally in the countryside, which could be thought reasonable to fly at. Rabbit, moorhen, hare, pheasant (if it gets up within 20 yards and the hawk is a male, usually so much faster than the female) the goshawk will try for anything if in good condition, or 'in yarak' as it is still called. This is a Persian word and has

A picture of myself, taken with Minerva when she
was 14 years old.

Mr. Geoffrey Pollard, one of the greatest exponents of grouse hawking that modern falconry has probably known, prepares to cast off a peregrine on the moors of Caithness, Scotland. The picture shows the manner of holding the falcon. The falcon has just been unhooded and stands for a moment getting her bearings and taking stock of the general situation. Out of the picture a pointer is steadily holding a point on a covey of grouse.

When the hawk takes off she will mount to her accustomed pitch before the grouse are flushed or 'served' to the hawk and, with any luck, she stoops and strikes one dead to the ground with her tightly clenched foot. She may attain a pitch or ceiling of 500–600 feet, or even more if she is a high flyer. On the stoop she may reach any speed up to 90–100 m.p.h. Much higher estimates of likely speeds are probably over optimistic.

persisted throughout the centuries. The goshawk will be termed to be 'in yarak' if in good order and ready to be taken out to fly. It is not applied to longwings.

All being well, she flies directly after the quarry. If she catches it, she 'binds' to it, in other words, clutches hold of it, killing it almost instantly by the massive claws sinking in like needles. The falconer then 'makes in' to her, which means going gently up to her, perhaps on his knees for the last few yards, taking her back on the glove, rewarding her with a titbit perhaps from the quarry, and carrying on for the next flight.

If she misses and the quarry escapes, the shortwing will probably either land on the ground in some anger and disgust, in which case she may be 'made in' to in the same way and taken up. Or she may swing away into a tree to see what is to happen next.

In theory, the hawker with the goshawk will call her back direct to his upheld fist, in which he holds a little piece of meat, by means of the whistle or special cry which he will always use when wanting his hawk to come back to him. The same cry or whistle can also be used whenever she is being fed, so that the two things are always associated in her mind.

We shall see later how to get her to do this and how to proceed if she declines to conform to copybook procedure. This is not unknown with a goshawk, as can well be imagined.

The longwing procedure is totally different, in that she is trained to start her operation at quarry, in most cases, from the air. She starts when already airborne, flying above 'waiting on' for her quarry to be produced by her falconer partner and perhaps his dog. When the quarry appears, she will in theory dive down on it in the famous longwing 'stoop', striking it down with the clenched foot used as a fist, taking off momentum by 'throwing up' into the air over the quarry which is now lying on the ground inert, and then dropping on to it preparatory to 'feeding up' on it. The falconer will then 'make in' in the same fashion as with the shortwing. She can also be flown from the fist, 'out of the hood', or 'at bolt', as it is called, direct at winged quarry, which often works very well.

But if she is airborne, and no quarry can be produced

Mr. Croft Slater's haggard saker, caught when a wild adult, was lost when she raked away, flying rooks in the south of England. The pattern of adult plumage does not change to the same extent as in some other hawks when they reach maturity.

at the crucial moment for her, she cannot be allowed to look about for something to chase herself, since it might be miles away, even out of sight. If she clears off, or 'rakes away' after this, contact can easily be lost and she vanishes, possibly never to be seen again. With the country now criss-crossed with roads, fences and other obstacles, it is by no means easy to follow a flying hawk.

In days gone by, the falconer followed at speed on horseback. Enclosures were fewer and it was half the fun dashing across the country in pursuit of the hawk. Such country can rarely be found these days and most people are not geared to following on horseback, although, of course, it is not entirely impossible to do in the right places.

But the hawk must be brought down from the air; holding up a fist and whistling will not do in this case. She is brought down to the 'lure', an object resembling the sort of quarry she usually flies at, perhaps a small leather pad with a couple of pheasant, duck or pigeon wings firmly fastened to it. It may even be a dead bird itself swung round on a cord, which must be more rewarding for the hawk to land upon. It is a matter of opinion whether it is best to use a dead bird or animal for the lure, instead of the more usual leather pad just described.

This is swung round the falconer's head on a long cord to attract the hawk's notice. Her special call, again a cry or whistle, is made. In theory she descends at once towards the lure and as she comes up to it, the falconer lets it drop to the ground perhaps six or ten paces from him. The hawk drops on to the lure which has something interesting on it for the hawk to pull at – perhaps a tough piece of leg or some such object which will not come off at once and be swallowed.

The falconer now makes in to her in exactly the same way as on the other occasions, taking her up off the lure on to his glove and perhaps rewarding her with some titbit.

To train the shortwing to operate correctly, it is only necessary to persuade her to come an increasingly long distance to reach you for her food from her outside perch.

Dr. Ridley McPhail's lanner with her quarry. Dr. McPhail is editor of *The Falconer*, the publication of the British Falconers' Club.

Roddy McKerracher, the Scottish talconer, above, holds a fine female goshawk before her first moult and, left, a kestrel demonstrates her friendliness with her young master.

The shikra, a female haggard, is a hawk formerly much used in India and still occasionally to be found in European hands.

To begin with this will be the length of the leash itself, which it is not necessary to untie at this stage. She can be fed with a very small feed two or three times a day, which gives the falconer perhaps three opportunities a day to increase the distance. But on each occasion she must not be asked to come more than three times, since she will soon get bored and over-wary and refuse the last time. This is a setback and you may have to go back to square one with her, making her come the shortest distance again and working up once more.

Two enthusiastic leaps or little flights towards you are worth much more than a very protracted wait for a longer distance effort.

Because she is going to fly to and from your fist, the shortwing must at this stage always be fed on your fist after she has done her exercise of coming to you off the perch. Do not be persuaded to leave the food at her perch for her to feed herself.

She will immediately consider that she can now feed for herself without your co-operation. Since this provision of food is your only link with her at all, it is vital that there should be no break in it. The same goes for the longwing.

As time goes on, the shortwing will come the full length of the leash at once, as soon as you call her and offer food.

She must now start coming further still. Get a long cord or twine, perhaps 50 yards at least. This is still called a 'creance' from the French word. When the day comes that you decide she will come say 10 yards, gently tie one end of the creance to the swivel at the end of the jesses, through the loop in which the leash passes. Undo the leash and remove it from the swivel. Walk quietly away with your back to the hawk, paying out the creance along the ground as you go, making sure not to pull on it by treading on it or snagging it on something on the ground. To jerk her off the perch by mistake at this stage could be a great setback.

At the end of the 10 yards turn towards her, hold up your gloved hand with a little bit of food in it, and call her. All being well, she will fly to you at once and

All hawks should be weighed every day, except perhaps during moulting, and an accurate note kept of the weight. In the case of small hawks, this should be to the nearest half ounce. A beginner should weigh his hawk without fail just before taking her out to fly, and any undue fluctuation is a sure sign that something is wrong. If she is overweight from her accustomed regular flying weight, there will be a strong chance of losing her. If more than a very little underweight, she may be starting some illness or be off colour and again it would be unwise to fly her. It is handy to keep a set of scales, like that in the picture, with the regular flying weight on it. When taking her out to fly, it then takes only a moment to set her gently down on the scales perch, hooded if necessary. You will be able to see at once whether she is at the right weight, without having to adjust the weights. Here, a tiercel laggar stands hooded for weighing.

land on your glove with a very satisfying motion.

The first time she comes this considerable distance it could be as well to give her a good feed and not ask her to repeat the performance straightaway.

The distance can be rapidly increased every day. Keep a chart of her daily weight: this is very important for all flying hawks. Their normal weight, either when fit for flying, or during non-flying periods, must be known. Any variation will indicate at once some conditions which may make it unwise to fly her. If she is not doing any flying, it will show that she is getting too fat to be healthy if her weight starts to go up, or if it goes down she may be sickening for something if her food has not been altered significantly in quality or quantity.

Weigh your hawk as soon as you get her. Any spring balance will do with a piece of wood screwed to the top in place of the usual pan. After some experience, and when the hawk can be guaranteed to stand quietly on a weighing scale, a balance scale may be preferred, with loose weights added to one side. They are more accurate on the whole. They have the advantage that if kept in one particular place, with the hawk's normal amount of weights left in position on the scale every day, it is possible to see easily and at once if her weight has in fact altered.

The spring balance is sometimes not too easy to read down to the half ounce which is needed, especially for the smaller hawks. It also tends to go up and down in a way disconcerting to a hawk, adding to the difficulty of getting an accurate reading. But like so many other things, it is a matter of opinion which is the best scale to use.

With the shortwing's weight remaining steady at a weight at which she seems to fly to you, the moment comes when you must let her fly a good distance, perhaps 50 or 100 yards, free, without the creance.

For the beginner, this is perhaps the supreme moment. It is the first time he is to have proof of whether his training has been correct. It is also the first time that the hawk has an unfettered opportunity of clearing off altogether, without so much as a backward glance. It is indeed a great moment. Even the experienced falconer will probably feel a special thrill the first time a new hawk flies free.

It is easier to get an assistant to carry her gently to a post the chosen distance off, while you stand by the perch. A gate or any perch will do, but try to arrange it in an open space with no inviting trees or other likely perches nearby. There is no point in putting such ideas deliberately into her head.

Try also to have no one else about other than you and your assistant: certainly no dogs, cars, onlookers or any other distractions. You will both need all your concentration.

Call her off in the normal way which you have done each of the preceding days. If she is 'in yarak' if a shortwing, or in the corresponding condition for a longwing, 'sharp set', and there is no unfortunate disturbance, she will come straight to you just as easily as if it had been 10 yards on a creance.

As she comes to you, hold your fist directly in her path, not out to one side. As soon as she has landed, slip the jesses through the eyelets – if wearing Aylmeri – and intertwine them between your second and third finger to get a good grip. She will start to feed on the large piece of prominently displayed food that you have held up as you called her off. Slip the jesses through and round the swivel, pull the leash through its swivel loop and wind the leash round your glove between the same fingers. Call it a day. Go back to her perch and set her down after she has had a good feed.

After this, take to calling her off at all sorts of distances up to 150 or even 200 yards. If you are doing this by yourself, she may fly after you as you walk away: you will hear by her bells that she is on the move. Turn and take her to the glove, but then try casting her into a nearby tree.

Let her swoop up into a branch of a single isolated tree and call her down out of it. Carry her about as much as you possibly can, and get her used to all manner of people, noises and events.

After you have got fully confident – perhaps five or six weeks from the time of getting her, perhaps a great deal less – you are ready to try her at a rabbit or some convenient quarry.

Colonel Carnie's goshawk closes rapidly on a jack rabbit, below and opposite.

If you are fortunate enough to have a dog to work with her, then the dog must have been sitting quietly with you throughout all her training. She will soon get used to the dog and probably quite understand that the dog will be helping her.

When ready to try for, perhaps, a rabbit, see first that her weight is the same, or a little less this time, as it has been for all her free flying.

Remove the perch jesses and put in the flying jesses, if using Aylmeri. Holding her securely with these – she may easily bate at something you have not noticed, so you must beware of her flying off unexpectedly – walk cautiously through the rabbit country. If the dog is working, she will watch closely as you move along. Try to get her first flight at a very close and easy rabbit.

As the rabbit springs up and she dashes at it, at the same instant let go the jesses. It seems unnecessary to stress letting go the jesses, but it is surprising how often the beginner does not let go at once. The hawk stops abruptly and dangles from the glove, upside down and furious. By the time the beginner has collected his wits, the rabbit has vanished. He now lets her go and she drops to the ground or flies off in vain pursuit. This is a bad start and discouraging for the bird. Make every effort to see she gets a kill of some sort on her first flight. This can usually be ensured if a little trouble is taken: it is very important and will greatly help the future flying career of the hawk.

After she has killed, wait until she has just 'broken in' to the rabbit before 'making in' very gently indeed, and on your knees for the last few paces.

Have a good piece of beef or chicken leg or something she specially likes in the glove. Interpose this between her and her rabbit so that as she goes down with her beak to get at the rabbit, the beef is right under her beak. She will with luck go for the beef and step up on to your glove.

Stand up slowly and, if you are not going to try another flight, hold the jesses firmly until you can change them to the permanent jesses, putting on swivel and leash and return home, allowing her to

113

In Hungary, Mr. Lorant de Bastyai's saker stoops
at a heron marauding the State Fisheries.

A sight many falconers go through a lifetime without ever seeing: a cast of peregrines are flown together, on this occasion, at a magpie on the Irish moors. Albert, the tiercel, has stooped and struck the magpie and is caught by the camera throwing up into the sky almost directly above. At the same instant, the falcon, Victoria, is peeling off above, and has started driving down on to the unfortunate magpie with that amazing combination of wing flicker and gravity which produces the most exciting spectacle in falconry – a peregrine's stoop. A highly skilled photographer, as well as falconer, Mr. John Morris has produced here a unique photograph.

feed as much as she wants on the beef or whatever food you had for her.

If you are sufficiently careful, you can with your free right hand, while still collecting her off the rabbit, cut off its head as it lies dead on the ground with a knife from your bag – a pair of kitchen scissors are almost more useful than a knife. There is less likelihood of accidentally cutting the hawk's toes. Substitute the rabbit's head for the beef and allow her to eat at the neck. You may have had a chance to split the rabbit's head open to allow the hawk to feed on the brain, which she will consider a special treat.

She is now manned, trained and entered. It only remains to get in as much practice as possible in all sorts of conditions, and to note down in a hawking diary every detail about her.

There will unfortunately be some occasion when the shortwing refuses to come back to the fist, but sits impassively in a tree, paying no attention.

In theory this will never happen. But in falconry, as in most things, theory and practice are not always coincident. The purist will stay with his moody goshawk until perhaps a matter of hours afterwards she does drop down on to the glove as if nothing untoward had ever occurred.

The falconer who cannot spare these hours may break the principles and long-established practice by producing from his bag a small leather or canvas object containing a couple of pounds of sand sewn into it, all about the size of a rabbit's body. Round this has been sewn a cured rabbit skin, head and all. He throws this out towards the goshawk still standing in her tree, upwind of her if there is any breeze, and at a shallow enough angle to enable her to glide comfortably on to it without having to do aerial contortions.

The stuffed rabbit has a swivel sewn on to it. To this he attaches his creance – perhaps he keeps one permanently attached to it for emergencies. He withdraws 20 yards or perhaps more and calls the hawk. At the same time, he twitches the rabbit along a few inches at a time.

If the hawk is remotely in flying order she will be unable to resist this and will very soon glide down on

to it. He then makes quietly in to her as if she had made a kill and takes her up with a beakful of reward, whatever his personal feelings as to how much she has deserved a reward.

If the hawk is not in flying order, she should not have been taken out in the first place.

Indication of her being ready to fly will be a rousing or fluffing of her feathers, her weight not above her regular flying weight, nor suddenly dropped three or four ounces below (if a goshawk – less, if a smaller hawk, of course), and a general air of well-being. If she stands chirping with feathers tight against her, she is not 'in yarak', and not ready to fly.

A goshawk in yarak usually has the small feathers on the back of her neck slightly raised. Many hawkers (hawkers for shortwings, falconers for longwings) will not fly a goshawk until she has 'roused' three times, in other words, fluffed up her feathers and given a good shake. It is a good principle.

The longwing preparation and training is very similar with two important differences. Firstly, she will need training to wear a hood. And secondly, as we have seen, she will need to be 'made to the lure', to fly to the lure instead of to the fist. She must also have regular exercising flights to the lure, which the shortwing does not need, and will not perform except under the greatest protest, and probably not more than once or twice.

The longwing must be invited to come to her feed to the lure as soon as she has got to the stage of coming to the fist up to the length of the leash. Her training must proceed on the same lines as the shortwing until after the final stages where she flies free for the first time. She must fly safely and directly when called off in the same manner before any work is started on making her fly round in the longwing manner.

The lure to which we have referred already, is ideally a leather pad stuffed with sand if the leather itself is not heavy enough. This makes an object which is heavy enough to be swung steadily round to attract the hawk, yet not so heavy that if the falconer inadvertently catches her a blow with it, as she flies to it, she does not suffer injury.

The lure needs, as has been mentioned, a swivel at the front end and a couple of pigeon or duck wings tied permanently and realistically to it, and leather or strong twine threads for tying a 'garnish' or piece of meat to it.

In emergency or indeed as a matter of course, as already mentioned, any dead bird like a pigeon can be used, with the line tied to the legs. If used as a general rule, it has constantly to be replaced through decay, and also is not half so easy to swing accurately when flying the hawk to it. If the hawk perhaps binds to it in the air above the falconer's head, she may easily tear a lump out of it and go off for a feed, which is disruptive and a nuisance. Nothing elaborate is needed, until enthusiasm drives the falconer to experiment with the American invention of artificial lure with jointed wings which flap when the lure is thrown up or swung.

With the longwing coming readily 50 yards to the swung lure, this is the time to start her real flying.

As she comes towards the lure which the falconer has swung out to lie on the ground a few paces in front of him, he twitches it away behind him. The hawk will instantly wheel off to the side or throw straight up into the air. She has started flying to the lure: it is a very exciting moment.

The first time she does this, the lure should be thrown out again at once in front and left there for her to land on and take a mouthful of the 'garnish'.

Do not fly again until the next session. This time it can be twitched away a second time, and perhaps more, according to her reactions.

At the first sign of her getting slow or bored, leave the lure out for her to land on. This is very exciting work and one of the greatest pleasures of hawking. Many people will say that no hawking experience compares with flying a keen hawk to the lure, it being even preferable to one fine stoop at quarry. That is over in seconds and it may not be possible to fly again that day, but flying to the lure can be done for much longer, depending on the fitness of the hawk.

She may be stooped 20 or 30 times at the lure before being taken up on it. The falconer soon becomes adept

Exercising a hawk at the lure is the most thrilling part of hawking, next to actually flying at quarry. The lure must be switched from side to side without hitting the hawk or allowing her to grasp or bind to it before the exercise period is over. It is very pretty to watch well done and skill soon develops with practice. It must not, of course, be carried out for too long at a time, yet long enough to exercise the hawk, which is a matter of judgement and experience.

Mr. Croft Slater's red-headed merlin, a haggard called Pepper, a native of India and parts of South Africa, below and opposite, was caught and trained when already an adult wild bird past the first moult. She was flown by Mr. Slater for two seasons, after which she was given to Mr. Tony Houston in Ireland, where she continued to add to her bag of a snipe, magpies and partridge. She was a very exceptional bird and was expertly trained and flown. In the picture below, Pepper, her crop ready to burst after a large feed, is wearing an Indian hood with Dutch bracing. She does not wear bells, as the merlin is too small to wear bells large enough to be effective. Because her nails do little harm, Mr. Slater is able to hold her without gloves. In some people's opinion, the feel of the bird's foot on the hand helps to preserve a bond between man and bird, but a glove would normally be worn when flying a merlin.

at working the lure to bring out the greatest flying powers of his hawk. Many hawks appear to love flying to the lure, diving at great speed. A cleverly worked lure feels magnificent to do and is superb to watch.

Anyone who has devoted himself solely to short-wings and has never flown a longwing to the lure has denied himself one of the greatest thrills in falconry, one of the most easily provided and most skilled to perform. No quarry is needed, no dog, no assistant, only a very small area of open ground, with no distractions.

The pictures on pages 117, 118 and 119 of a laggar at work shows this well. The laggar, particularly good at flying to the lure, banks sharply close to the ground and drives hard at ground level, before throwing up over the falconer, preparatory to another burst of speed perhaps from 100 feet up.

As the falconer becomes more experienced and knows his hawk with greater intimacy, he can give himself a brilliant and exciting few minutes, and his hawk most excellent exercise, bringing her to and keeping her in, a peak of condition.

Constant flying and stooping to the lure will, however, have the effect of making the hawk 'lure bound', only interested in flying to the lure, and gradually less use for flying at quarry. This needs guarding against, since the temptation to fly a long-wing solely at the lure can become very strong. But it is far better than not flying her at all.

A really fit hawk will keep stooping and flying at a lure for a surprising time. Walter Joynson, the well known Scottish falconer, has had a hawk stoop over 90 times from varying heights without her becoming tired, and yet have her dash and determination at live quarry quite undiminished. Prolonged flying at the lure does not therefore necessarily prove detrimental, but such an operation as Mr. Joynson's, needs the greatest skill and experience.

In former times, a hawk could be prevented from becoming lure bound by throwing up a live pigeon or some other bird after a prolonged period of flying to the lure, so that the hawk knew she was expected to catch her food and not rely entirely on a well

A variety of hoods: at the top is a traditional
Dutch or European hood with Dutch bracings, the
long ones to close the hood firmly yet not
uncomfortably on the hawk's head, the short ones
to slacken or 'strike' the hood. The hoods in the
centre and at the bottom are in the traditional
Indian pattern and those on the left and right are
Indian-pattern hoods with Dutch bracing, a method
much favoured by modern falconers.

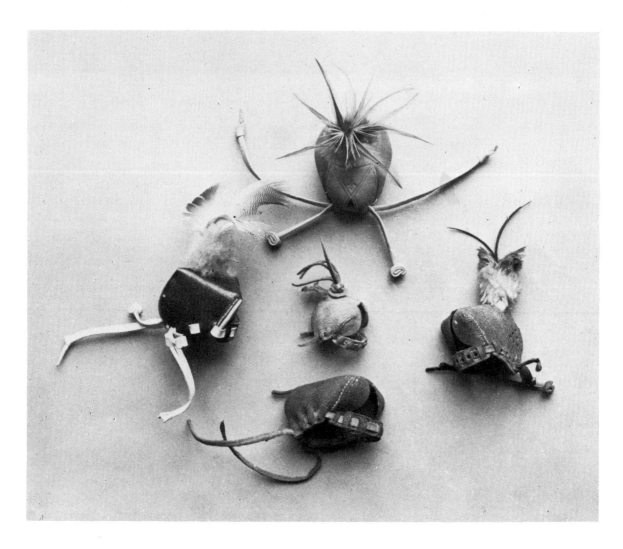

garnished lure. This practice is frowned on in Britain and is not used. It is a good thing to try to prevent a set pattern from developing when flying at the lure, and to keep as much variety as possible. But this is not easy, since there is very little scope for variety.

Nowadays of course, at least in Britain, opportunities are limited and a longwing may have to make do with very restricted flying. The falconer has to depend to a great extent on lure flying.

To encourage her to wait on above him, in other words, to mount up and wait for him to put out the lure or to serve her with wild quarry for her to fly at, the falconer may cast her off from his fist and not put out the lure at once.

This needs doing carefully, since if she sees no lure at once she may streak off to look for something else.

The falconer has the lure always ready to swing. He shows it briefly to the hawk to keep her in his immediate vicinity, but withdraws it, perhaps holding it close to him. The hawk will want to get at the lure if she is in proper condition and will usually start flying round in small circles above the falconer.

By constant practice he can encourage her to stay very much above him with just a glimpse of the lure now and again if her attention begins to wander.

The hood

A kestrel, goshawk or merlin seldom needs a hood, but is frequently provided with one. The longwing needs to be hooded, particularly when travelling. Most beginners will want to hood their hawk whether she needs it or not, partly for the interest of such a traditional and integral part of the hawk's equipment, and partly for the brave show a hawk can make wearing a gaily plumed hood.

An experienced falconer, interested only in the condition and flying ability of his hawk, will not concern himself with whether she makes a brave show or not. But there is no point in trying to deny that many people are perhaps initially attracted to the whole sport by the appearance of some finely hooded hawks and wish to know more about the whole subject of falconry.

There is no harm in this. But it must be borne in mind that the hood is first and foremost a means of allowing an otherwise nervous and highly strung hawk to stand about or to be transported peacefully without being upset by every new movement or noise about her, or from wanting to get after every bird which she sees as she stands on her block in the weathering ground.

As soon as the beginner receives a longwing, he should 'make her to the hood' – in other words, get her used to wearing a hood. Before she arrives he will have bought a hood of the right type for her from one of the addresses in the back of this book. After some experience, he will know whether it is a good fit or not and will have tried to make one himself. He will be entitled to congratulate himself if he has any success in this direction at all.

The hood should fit closely, but without discomfort, and be so well fitting that all light is excluded from the hawk's eyes, which is the sole object of the hood. Whichever is used, the hawk must be made to accept it without demur.

A useful beginning for a new young hawk is a soft leather hood, called a rufter, which is extremely comfortable and allows the hawk to feed easily while wearing it.

All hoods have a brace at the back to tighten or slacken it when on the hawk, except the true Indian pattern. Here the lace runs right round the bottom of the hood and is drawn in close enough to keep it on the individual hawk for which it is used. The loops grip the lace and there is no provision for loosening completely, or 'striking' the hood once it is on. It comes off easily and is equally simple to put on.

The Dutch method has two large pairs of braces, one for tightening and one for loosening. The longer braces are for closing the hood tight enough to avoid it being scratched or shaken off, yet not so tight as to be uncomfortable. The shorter braces are for loosening the hood in order to 'strike' or take off the hood. Once on the hawk's head, the falconer, since he only has one free hand – the hawk being on the other – leans forward, takes the appropriate brace on the far side with his right hand, catches the nearest one with his teeth and gives a quick light pull. It takes a little practice to perfect, but putting the hood on is not so easy.

Some people never become proficient at it. They seem unable to be gentle and quick enough. The hawk anticipates the fumbling and discomfort: she bobs, weaves, ducks and swerves until the inexpert falconer crams the hood over her beak and with his middle fingers forces her head through into the hood. This will make her thoroughly 'hood-shy', and is a disaster. The effects on a hawk of this being done a few times can well be imagined.

The secret is lightness, dexterity, and practice, coupled with a favourite snack or feed up every time the hood is put on to begin with. After a short period, of course, no reward is necessary each time since the hawk will be so used to the hood that it becomes part of her daily life.

A new hawk can be hooded to begin with in the half light. Hold the hood tightly by the plume below and in front of her head, so that she sees something there which does not suddenly take her by complete surprise. Slip her beak through the beak opening in the hood, at the same time revolving your left arm anti-clockwise. This will have the effect of making her put her head down and forward a fraction to maintain her balance. The hood, if of Dutch brace pattern, will have had the braces opened to slacken the back of the hood. The hood will then slip over her head quite easily. Pushed gently into place, and the relevant braces tightened by hand and teeth, the hawk may scratch at the hood and try to shake it off. But she soon gets quite used to it, provided it is a comfortable fit and has not been harshly put on.

Practice is the answer for the falconer. The long-wing can be taken about in cars or in assorted company and set down where there are people about, undisturbed through the darkness of her hood. She will stay calm and unflustered as long as hooded.

She can keep on a comfortable hood for long periods without discomfort. She may feed through a hood which is not too tight and stay for a matter of hours hooded without harm.

The goshawk and the others ought to be so accustomed to all sights and sounds that they are unperturbed by them. The hood is therefore unnecessary. But every falconer ought to be able to hood a hawk. It is not a good enough excuse to maintain that he flies only a goshawk and therefore does not need to use a hood.

It will be understood that this is the merest outline of how the beginner is to get his hawk, long or short wing, flying. The object is to get started without being bogged down in consideration of the endless details which need taking into account in all the different aspects of hawking.

Moulting

Hawks moult their plumage each year, taking some months to drop and renew as many feathers as they are going to, which is of course not every single feather on their body.

The wing and tail are the important ones. They are dropped out in matching pairs one at a time, from

Above: a painting by the great bird artist, George Lodge, in 1896, shows the setter, Pero, coming suddenly upon the peregrine falcon, Duchess, who has just killed a snipe. This is quite a rare feat for any hawk other than a hobby or possibly a merlin. Duchess is startled at Pero's unexpected appearance round the rock, and takes off with the snipe, instead of staying with it on the ground where she could easily be taken up by the falconer and prepared for the next flight. But in this case, which was an actual incident, Duchess went off about two miles with the snipe (which is called 'carrying' and is, of course, a very undesirable habit), and took stand in a dead treetop. There she leisurely 'plumed' or plucked the snipe and consumed it, out of range of the whistling and lure-waving of the falconer. After this, she swung away down the wind and was not recovered until four days later.

Right: this intermewed tiercel Peale's falcon was killed, while weathering peacefully on his block, by a passing horned owl who took him unawares – a tragedy and a great loss.

Four different types of hoods: below, two Dutch
hoods; opposite, two Indian hoods.

alternate sides, in order not to destroy the balance of flight too much. The moult will generally start about May and go on until August or September, but it is impossible to say exactly since each bird may react differently to the food and general conditions. Birds in captivity may always moult at different times, perhaps slowly starting in February or March and dragging on over the whole summer and only completing it (if completed at all that year) in November or December.

The aim is to get the moult through as quickly as possible, since the falconer will probably want to fly his bird in August. To get this done, the hawk can either be left loose in a large loft or room for the whole summer, as soon as hawking has finished for the season. Or she can be kept on her perch and moved out every day, much as when she was in training, but not flying. She will be given as much food as she will finish up at one meal, her weight will be much higher than normal, and she will get quite fat. She cannot under these conditions be flown. If released, she would pay no attention to lure or outheld gloves, and she would be lost at once.

But before flying her it is not necessary for her complete suit of new feathers to have grown down. Feathers rarely get injured in ordinary flights.

When August arrives, her food must gradually be cut down, occasional washed meat given to her (which is meat soaked for 24 hours in water to get rid of the goodness of it without losing the bulk), and she will gradually become keener and ready to fly again.

There are various drugs suitable for hawks which tend to accelerate the moult. But they are a study on their own: many falconers are averse to giving their hawks any form of drug except as a last resort in serious illness. The European climate is not conducive to the success of constant physicking and drugging, such as practised in India, or used to be practised. With Indian falconers it was an obsession. European falconers have their own favourite ways of hastening a moult. Keeping the hawk in artificial light for most of the 24 hours, perhaps under an infra-red lamp, has given good results without apparently causing the

hawk discomfort. A diet including a high proportion of mice, rats, egg yolk, day old chicks – some things achieve results with some hawks which do no good to others. A sun-warmed loft to moult in is as good a treatment as any, with a large variety of food. A change of food can sometimes stimulate a moult, or reactivate one which appears to have stagnated.

One way of hastening the moult is suggested in the first of *Two Treatises on Falconry*, published by Quaritch, London, 1968, the second of which is D. C. Phillott's *Baz Nama*. This is a diet of hedgehogs boiled in milk and is one of the least extraordinary of dozens of different feeds of increasing absurdity and complexity – 'Dry the heart of three tigers and pound to a fine dust. Add the milk of a young human mother and give as a paste.'

The bird hatched in the summer of one year will not, of course, start to moult that same year. That is the reason why eyasses of the year are so much in demand for flying that same autumn, since they have a complete suit of feathers that whole year, while birds of a year and older are short of feathers due to their moulting. The eyass can therefore keep going all summer with flying at the lure and such like, although hawking for quarry will not start until things come into season for being flown at in August or later.

Food and medicine

Every ordinary hawk needs roughage in her food at least twice a week. This means the fur or feather of whatever is available. This churns round inside her, keeping the crop and pannel, or stomach, walls from becoming lined with harmful mucus. After a few hours this is thrown up in the form of a casting or pellet. If she is kept hooded for any length of time after a feed containing castings, she may not be able to open her beak wide enough to throw out the casting, so this possibility has to be borne in mind.

More hawks probably become ill and die through over-feeding and the giving of medicines than from any disease. A goshawk for instance should be given a gorge, or complete blow-out, eating herself to a

An albino red-tailed hawk, a bird of rare beauty, now intermewed, so throwing true albino.

standstill, at least once a week. Once a week also she should go without food at all, provided the weather is not very taxing with cold, rain and wind.

Longwings benefit from an occasional gorge, but should not be left so long without food.

Hawks suffer from one or two main troubles. Coughs and colds are easily picked up, leading to a condition where she spits up the foul smelling and slimy contents of her undigested crop.

Before administering a drug or ringing a vet, make an infusion of rhubarb by boiling some down, or the roots if not in season, and get her to take some by putting it down her throat with an eye-dropper.

A cold from her nares, or nostrils, can usually be checked by painting on her beak and over her nares some aromatic oil such as eucalyptus, with a small paint brush.

The biggest danger is one of the various forms of worm infestation. The hawk may go off her feed, or eat in a half-hearted way, perhaps flicking the food about. She may have diarrhoea, with her excrement (or mutes) not sliced firmly out but dribbled down the perch or block. These troubles should be noticed at once. If anything appears wrong, stop giving any castings and feed her on strips of fresh beef with a little thoroughly clean river sand rolled into it. This should put her right, coupled with best quality, easily digestible food in narrow strips. Perhaps pigeon's breast as a variant, but the great thing is to get her eating again if she is off her food.

Do not leave it too long. If you can make no progress, then you must get on to the nearest vet you can find who has a particular interest in birds. One of the scores of new drugs now available may very well cure her. On the other hand, it has never been more true than with hawks to say that prevention is better than cure. My experience is that hawks have a hard job to fight against the usually debilitating effects of a modern drug, almost as much of a battle as against the ailment itself, and drugs should be the very last resort.

Good food in as much variety as possible, clean surroundings, no damp or draughts, no over-feeding – all this should help to prevent illness.

As far as the goshawk is concerned, boredom, loneliness and isolation can destroy her spirit almost as effectively as a creeping illness can destroy her physique. Keep her daytime perch in as busy a place as possible, with all manner of people, children, cars, bicycles or whatever clattering about all the time. If you are alone, put her where she can see you coming and going all the time.

A vigorous mind is a great stimulant to a healthy body and should be looked after with equal care.

Longwings do not like such a hurly-burly, but should still be kept interested in life as much as possible, not marooned in a gloomy corner. This tends to make them less apprehensive when handled and accordingly better fliers.

In my experience, all hawks should be flown in as high conditions as is possible, in other words, as heavy as they could naturally be if they were getting as much food of the right sort in the wild as they wished. It therefore needs a little careful experiment to see how high you can get your hawk before you begin to lose contact. Experience will tell very quickly, but the beginner must feel his way slowly, otherwise he has soon lost his hawk altogether.

Some hawks like an occasional drink, even if it is only a mouthful of bath water. Here Colonel Carnie's goshawk treats himself to some refreshment on a hot morning.

Bath

Most hawks like to have a bath sometimes, but as with human beings some like it more often than others. It should always be available for a hawk, and any sort of container big enough for the hawk to stand with outstretched wings in four or five inches of water will suffice. If the outdoor perch can be put by a garden pool, this makes a very good bath, provided there is a ramp or stone to stand on at the right depth if the rest of the pool is too deep.

Some hawks like to walk in until the water is over their shoulders, while others will never go in more than two or three inches. A merlin of mine, kept for two years before being hacked back, would rarely have a bath more than once a week whatever the weather. A visiting eagle lay permanently in sun-warmed water during the day, so there is no accounting for tastes.

Although a bath should always be available, it is inadvisable for a hawk to be allowed to take a bath after about four o'clock, for fear she does not dry out completely before going to roost for the night. It is an easy way to catch a chill, since she is not free to fly round to dry herself and may be standing in a draught afterwards. Some hawks like to sip water now and again, and do this during a bath. But a hawk can go quite readily without any drinking water being available. I have never provided a hawk with any.

Bent feathers

After a journey in a confined space, a hawk's tail can easily get bent, and look as if it is going to stay that way. The wings sometimes suffer in the same way, but not so often.

There is an easy remedy for this. Hood the hawk, if she is made to the hood. If she is not and is not well manned enough to stand while you deal with her, put her in her mews on the screen perch in a very dull light. Get a wide deep jug, fill it with hot, but not boiling water.

Then either raise the jug up behind her so that her tail goes into the water, or if she is on the fist, lower

Imping a broken feather: the feather on the left has lost its tip and it is not worth doing anything about it. The one next to it is severely damaged, with the spine broken right across and the end half only just hanging on. This can easily happen when the hawk is flying quarry, when she is on the block or perch with the leash perhaps riding up and doing the damage, or when she bates along the top of the perch.

A broken feather must be attended to at once, since not only is the hawk's manoeuvrability affected, but the feathers on either side of the new gap will also begin to suffer. The hawk must either be put in a sock or stocking with the toe cut off to allow the hawk's head through lest she suffocate, or she must be tranquillised with Equinal or some similar harmless drug.

The missing or broken piece of feather must be matched up as near as possible with a piece of another feather. All major feathers which a hawk moults should be kept for just this purpose; it is then not difficult to cut off a piece of the right length from an exactly equivalent feather. But if you have not had your hawk through a moult, you will have to use a feather from another bird which will match up. It may have to be one from a crow or some sort of barnyard fowl, which will look odd and almost certainly be too soft, but it is better than nothing.

First cut the lower end of the new feather into a notch to fit the corresponding V cut in the broken feather. File a point at both ends of a piece of wire and stick one end about a third of an inch down the new piece of feather, see third feather from the left in the picture. Put a drop of a good waterproof glue on the wire, then slide the wire with its piece of feather up the spine of the existing feather until the feather becomes one piece again, as shown on the right of the picture.

Also illustrated in the picture, at the top, are two shaped files used for coping beaks. These are very useful, but if they cannot be found in an ironmongers, any other small file or nail file will do the job just as well.

her tail into it.

Do not give a long soak, but put the tail in and out a few times and the feathers will straighten. The same applies to a wing, although there will, of course, be more manoeuvring over a wing than a tail.

This is also a good method for cleaning a tail, or for removing bands of sticky paper which have been put on to save the feathers from any possible damage during a journey.

Broken feathers

A wing feather will very rarely get broken. A tail feather will break far more easily, especially on a shortwing who spends much more time on the ground and tends to have more ground level battles, and also to enter undergrowth after quarry.

A hawk's manoeuvrability is of course greatly affected by missing or broken tail feathers. For a goshawk, it is essential to have a full tail if the sudden twists and turns are to be made of which the hawk is so brilliantly capable.

The condition of the beak of Mr. George Mussared's recently acquired lanneret, below right, contrasts sharply with that of his goshawk in the picture on page 97. The beak needs coping, or trimming. The tip is too long, making eating difficult, since food gets impaled on the over-long hook. This can be remedied by gently scraping the beak tip into a better shape with a sharp penknife, being careful not to split the end of the beak, otherwise a crack will form which is very difficult to cure. Every mealtime a little food will be forced into the crack which will have to be cleaned, and this all adds up to a lot of trouble.

Worse is the condition of the side of the upper mandible, where the incorrect level of the two mandibles, coupled with unchecked growth has resulted in a large flake developing, beginning to split off along the beak. Regular tirings, which are birds' wings, tough bones still with scraps of meat to pull at, or any feed which needs to be torn and wrestled with, keep the beak in trim.

This beak must be pared as deftly as possible, preserving the notch or ledge, but making sure that no vestige of split remains to work up into the mandible. The hawk will have to be held firmly in a sock by an assistant while the operation is performed. A tranquilliser could be given if the hawk is particularly liable to be upset. Once in proper shape, regular tirings should preserve the natural outline of the beak.

Any such feathers found to be broken must be mended. This is not as difficult as it sounds, and is called 'imping', one of the few individual terms still used regularly and without affectation.

The hawk will have to be 'mailed', another term still used for slipping a sort of stocking or sock over a hawk, with the toe piece cut out for her head and her wings and legs stretched out at the back. She lies therefore in a bundle, very usefully trussed up for sending on a short journey (she would get cramp if for too long) or for lying her down to perform some operation such as imping, or 'coping' her beak, which means trimming an overlong or cracked beak to the right shape.

The sock must fit tightly enough to keep her wings close to her body and her legs stretched straight. If it is slack enough for her to get legs or wings up inside the sock, the last state will be far worse than the first, and you will be in a great mess.

To cope the broken feather, it is necessary to get another feather that can be made to replace the broken piece. Preferably, it will be one of the hawk's own

This decayed old goshawk, shot in Scotland in 1830, is believed to have been one of the last naturally free birds. To judge by the length of its beak, the goshawk must have been living on slops. Britain now again has a small population of wild goshawks, mostly built up from birds lost by falconers, and it is possible that they may re-establish themselves in some more remote districts.

feathers which she has moulted, a feather from the same position in the year before. All feathers should therefore be kept from year to year, in mothproof places. But if you do not have this, then get a feather of any other sort, perhaps of a rook or other bird, or indeed anything of the right size; it is preferable to have a feather of the wrong colour than to leave the gap, since the feathers on either side of it will be in danger of breaking, too.

Cut the break with a razor blade or very sharp knife so that it forms a neat V-shape. Cut the new feather the right length to make the broken feather now match the rest of the tail. Make a slot in the new piece to receive the V of the old stump. Take a small piece of wire or light metal the size of half a matchstick, or a fraction smaller than the bore of the shaft of the old feather and the new piece. Finely coat the wire with any strong waterproof glue, push it half up the shaft of the new piece of feather. Then push the other end of the wire with its piece of feather up the shaft of the existing feather on the hawk's tail or wing. By pushing it up carefully and level, it should be possible to make a

join so close that apart from any discrepancy in colour, the join can hardly be noticed. If a moulted feather is being used, the difference will not be detected at all except when very closely examined.

If a hawk breaks a feather which is still 'in the blood', which means it is still growing down and the shaft is not yet firm and empty of blood, the broken piece may bleed. This must be stopped.

Obviously it is not a suitable case for imping. Instead, a small plug of cottonwool with a very small section of a matchstick, or something similar, can be put up the broken shaft. This usually checks the bleeding. The feather may go on growing as if nothing had happened, but is far more likely either to stop growing for that moult, or to come out.

If it comes out, and there is bleeding from the socket, a piece of rice gently pressed into the socket as a plug will often stop the bleeding. No new feather will probably grow from there during that moult. This is an argument against taking up a hawk from her moult before she is 'hard penned', meaning before all her new feathers are fully down and hard in the quill, not soft with blood still in the shaft.

Coping: beak or nails too long

If a hawk does not get enough tough and bony food, her beak gets too long. She may then find difficulty eating her food since everything gets impaled on the over-long, over-sharp beak, and there is great danger of the upper mandible splitting. Like sand crack in a horse's hoof, this is a great nuisance and proves very difficult to cure.

Prevention is the remedy, by paring the beak with a penknife if it looks like getting too long.

Likewise nails can become too long or sharp, giving trouble by keeping a toe at too high an angle when on a block, or by piercing the sole of the foot when the foot is raised. Snip the tips off with a nail cutter, being sure it is sharp, or you may find the whole toenail splitting up much of its length.

Too soft a perch at night and the same for daytime block or perch can lead to over-long claws.

CHAPTER 9

It is fashionable these days to draw up Codes of Conduct for most activities in which people wish to indulge, and to invite all those interested in the subject to profess their adherence to the rules.

This is widely accepted: the Countryside Code encourages countryside users not to bring other users into disrepute by irresponsible or damaging behaviour in the countryside.

Falconers are apparently no exception and need a Code of Conduct as well. The issue of such a code does, of course, serve an additional purpose to that of laying down the law to club members and, by inference, to all who wish to train and fly hawks, whether club members or not.

This purpose is to show that falconers in general are a responsible body of people pursuing their interest in humane, sensible and law-abiding manner. This tends to give more authority to any appointed spokesmen who take up matters affecting falconry with government, local government or private concerns. It is one more reason why anyone with an interest in hawks and hawking should seek to join a club and lend more power to the spokesmen of the sport.

So what does the code consist of? It is largely a question of using commonsense. The first paragraph of the code issued by the British Falconers' Club, and widely agreed upon in this country and abroad, defines falconry. It is: 'The sport of taking wild quarry in its natural state and habitat by means of trained hawks.'

Falconry is normally synonymous with hawking, although many prefer to describe the use of a short-wing as hawking, reserving the more grandiloquent term of falconry for the longwings. The majority of regular fliers of hawks call the whole subject hawking, and all their birds hawks.

The definition is not as straightforward as it seems. Formerly in Britain, and still in countries abroad, it was and is the custom to release quarry out of bags or boxes at which hawks can be flown. Quarry might also be harboured in special cover to be flushed as required when each hawk is ready. This approximates to driving hares into country behind the slips in order that pairs of greyhounds may be shown a hare

This picture shows a remarkable occurrence at the Irish mews of the noted falconer, Mr. Ronald Stevens, author of the unforgettable book, *Laggard,* and of *Observations on Hawking*. For the second year, Mr. Stevens's peregrine tiercel has mated or 'coupled' with Mr. John Morris's saker falcon, Farah. The resultant healthy offspring are seen at their 'eyrie' at Mr. Stevens's home. (The survivor from the previous year's mating is shown in the picture on page 149.) This must be one of the most interesting and potentially valuable developments in the modern hawking world, since it holds out a real hope of being able to breed more and more hawks for the possible use of falconers. It will be most interesting to see how they develop. Mr. Phillip Glasier's Falconry Centre in Gloucestershire, in conjunction with the Hawk Trust, has also done much research and practical work on this aspect of hawk breeding in captivity, and the results are very encouraging.

A page from the hawking diary of Capt. J. Bell-Irving, the noted Scottish falconer, which he has kindly allowed me to reproduce, is of the greatest interest, showing the results of a visit to his Scottish estate by a party of falconers from Germany. It was a shortwing meet, all the hawks being goshawks, with the exception of Capt. Bell-Irving's Harris's hawk. It is a powerful bird from the south west of the United States and South America, and a vigorous flyer of all quarry.

A page from a Hawking Diary

An international shortwing meet of falconers from Westphalia, Germany held by invitation of Capt. and Mrs. J. Bell-Irving, at White Hill and Leafield, Dumfriesshire, in August, 1971. Eleven goshawks and one Harris's hawk flew on four days

Name	Hawk	Rabbit	Pheasant	Blue Hare	Brown Hare	Waterhen	Total Bag	Approximate flying weight in grammes
W. Bednarek	F. eyass gos.	6	½	—	—	1	7½	1060–1120
W. Bruns	F. eyass gos.	6	1	—	—	—	7	1000
H. Mussmann	F. eyass gos.	12	—	—	—	—	12	1080
J. Bell-Irving	F. eyass gos. 1970	3	½	1	—	—	4½	920
J. Hebbeler	F. eyass gos. 1970	not flown	1	3	1	—	5	1050
A. Huster	F. eyass gos. 1969	4	—	2	—	—	6	1050–1100
P. Rade	F. passage gos. 1970	7	—	2	—	—	9	1060
H. Schröder	F. eyass gos. 1960	5	—	—	—	—	5	1200
R. Cappellaro	M. eyass gos. 1967	6	—	—	—	—	6	640
G. Krych	M. eyass gos. 1967	4	—	—	—	—	4	630
Mrs. J. Mitchell	M. eyass gos. 1970	—	—	not flown	—	—	—	610
Mrs. J. Bell-Irving	F. eyass gos. 1969 Harris's Hawk	1	—	1	—	—	2	880
12	12	54	3	9	1	1	68	

throughout the day in the one place. Hawks entered in the continental manner are often better trained and become more rapidly efficient. But the practice of releasing bagged quarry for any activity is not now acceptable in Britain, and might even be thought to be against the law. Whether or not this is the case, it is now against the Falconry Code of Conduct and is not done by British falconers.

The next paragraph declares that the keeping of hawks as pets is not falconry, and is contrary to accepted practice.

Many people think it unfair and a waste of a hawk to keep it in an enclosure or tied up to perch or block month in and month out without ever flying it, or trying to train it in any way. There is much of this done, and in most cases it is regrettable. But there are many occasions when no harm is done, as with hawks which have something serious and permanently wrong with them which will prevent them ever being entered as trained hawks, or from being 'hacked back' or returned to the wild. In such a case, it would be quite excusable to keep the bird and preserve its health and life as long as possible. Most falconers would not want to keep the bird themselves under these conditions, but would be very averse to destroying the hawk on realizing that it would never be fit to fly.

Some hawks also prove themselves unwilling, or possibly unable for some unidentifiable reason, to fly at live quarry. They prefer restricting their flying to a few circuits round their master and partner, and to return after a very short time to his fist for food and the warmth and security of a mews. Here is a case for someone who would like a hawk as a pet: they can make very nice pets. But the new owner would not consider himself a falconer and would not wish to be thought of as one.

Under the next paragraph, code readers are urged to: 'endeavour by all means to promote the welfare and future survival of hawks in the wild state in a world where modern developments are increasingly unfavourable to their future.'

It would be very shortsighted of anyone interested in hawking not to do this. It is also an injunction not to be selfish by taking more birds than are strictly needed out of the general world population of hawks. This does get overlooked: three eyries in the north of England were denuded of their total of seven eyasses during the 1972 season by a self-professed falconer, a case of sheer greed and blatantly illegal. Such action is not that of anyone who has the general good of falconry at heart. It is unfortunately true that this sort of behaviour has to be borne in mind when making a code for falconry. The making of the code or of the law itself has no direct effect on preventing the robbery, since neither are enforceable to the extent of being able to prevent it. But a collective disapproval expressed by the majority of other falconers would tend to discourage one who wished to take part in illegal hawking activities.

There is an increasing trend for people who are not specifically interested in falconry to establish aviaries and wild life collections. The number of these throughout the country is growing. Many of them are a natural market for birds of prey illegally taken and sold with no questions asked. They may well be the reason, apart from birds being sold abroad, for the very considerable increase of robbing during the past few years.

The code goes on to remind its readers that they are: 'under both a legal and a moral obligation to observe the laws and customs of the United Kingdom and of foreign countries with regard to the taking, import and export of hawks, the taking of quarry species and the right of access to land in the country concerned.'

No responsible person should need reminding of this: it is regrettably true that anyone about to break any of the laws and customs is not going to desist in reading in a code of conduct that he ought not to break the law. But it is worth reminding such a person that if he were a member of a club, he could not expect to remain so after being detected in some deliberate illegality of this nature. It is clear that the great majority of people breaking the laws in this respect are not interested in hawking, but only in selling the birds for which the demand is growing.

The code then sets out some basic facts described as the 'Ethics of care and training of hawks'.

(1) hawks must be properly housed, fed, equipped, trained and exercised,

(2) no more hawks should be kept than can be properly cared for, and

(3) a falconer should only keep a hawk if he can be sure of giving it adequate flights in suitable country at suitable quarry.

It also adds that: 'every endeavour must be made to recover a lost hawk.' Hawks sometimes escape through a leash or swivel, or even part of a perch breaking, and fly off trailing a long piece of leather. This, of course, is a disaster, since the bird will be bound to get tangled up very soon and starve to death. It will be most likely to hang helplessly upside down, in which case death comes very soon.

This possibility is a nightmare for any falconer. Most hawks are probably lost owing to something breaking, or even a knot coming untied. This latter event should certainly never happen and there can be no excuse for it. The knot should be tied at least twice if the leash is at all dry. It is a good habit to get into the automatic tying of a knot several times. Some Chinese illustrations to a hawking treatise show very elaborate knots several inches long: the decorative and ceremonial effect disguises the practical sense in tying a knot which cannot possibly come undone.

Hawks have also been lost by suddenly bating off or taking fright at the exact moment in between the falconer having taken her off her perch or block and having settled her, properly secured, on his glove. It is mortifying to see a hawk, perhaps not yet trained, flying off with all her jesses, swivel and leash dangling below. Any falconer who at the end of his days can cross his heart and say this has never happened to him even once has been more careful than most.

As with all such incidents, there is no excuse for them being allowed to happen. They just do sometimes happen. There is nothing to be done except hope to be able to run after her and keep her in sight, and trust that she will catch in a fence or low branch very quickly. The disturbance of all the gear hanging below

may prevent a trained hawk swinging back at once to the lure, but anything is worth trying to avert the imminent disaster of a high tangle. On such an occasion, a falconer will need no urging to 'make every endeavour' to retrieve her.

The code goes on: 'Hawks that are no longer required must either be handed on to a falconer who will treat them in accordance with the Code, or be returned to the wild . . . in good feather, high condition and reasonably capable of killing for itself.'

This is to discourage hawks being sold for aviaries or needlessly to become pets. But they should not be hacked back (or returned to the wild) if they are not a native species, since their chance of survival would in that case be negligible. It is hard enough for a native hawk to stay alive: an exotic bird would have even less chance.

Returning a hawk to the wild, or introducing it if it has never experienced a free life, does not consist of merely taking the hawk to what seems suitable country and letting her go. Unless she has done a lot of killing after training – and not always even then – she may not get down at once to the serious business of killing for her own food. She may well be so used to being fed by the falconer that the actual killing is not firmly enough linked in her mind with her own survival. The result of this could be that she leaves it too long before she realizes she must get something to eat. If nothing turns up very soon her strength may start to wane and either with it, or before that, her will and determination to make a kill. Bad weather may coincide with this situation, and she becomes so seriously reduced in killing power that she starves to death.

With adult birds this is an unlikely chain of events, but it can easily happen with young hawks.

The solution is simple. It entails feeding her up with food tied to a board or other object in the place you propose to release her. Immediately after feeding up, which should be in the late evening, she is likely to select a roosting place nearby for the night. As soon as she has left the hack-board, fresh food must be tied in the same place. It has to be tied to prevent her

An eagle with his owner at St. Hubert, Belgium.

Robin Haigh with his intermewed eyass steppes eagle, below and opposite, affectionately known as The Lump because of the awful burden of carrying him. He flies at 5lb 8oz and regularly takes a variety of quarry. 'I do not carry him like an ordinary hawk,' says Mr. Haigh, 'but throw him off and work towards him. He will follow for literally miles without having to be shown the lure, a technique that should not under any circumstances be tried by the beginner.

carrying it away a good distance, so that the point of having food ready in exactly the same place every time, and only capable of being consumed on that spot, is not lost.

The next morning she may come down for an early feed to the hack-board again. She may then, after a digesting period, 'putting over her crop' as it is called, search about, perhaps rather vaguely, for some quarry or other.

If she leaves it too late to find any that day, she will already have had a meal twice on the same spot and so will know that it is worth looking there again. Since the falconer has replenished the board, she gets a feed again. Food should be put out morning and evening. When she starts to become successful in killing, she will gradually come back to the board less and less

often. After a couple of days continued absence, it is safe to assume that if she has not been shot or trapped, she is fending for herself.

But if she is not being released on your land, it is important not just to select what you think is a likely district for her to thrive in and set up the hack-board without anyone knowing or being told.

To give her every chance, especially while she is still at the stage of thinking and taking it for granted that all human beings are kindly disposed towards her, it is important that local people should be told about the impending release. It may not be easy to find a good district for her where the people round about can be trusted with the information.

If this cannot reasonably be found, it would be wrong to arrange her hacking back at all. There are

Left: Mr. J. McFarlane's Arabian passage lanner,
caught during migration before the first moult, is
on the point of starting the second moult.

Leopard, a North American peregrine falcon.

always people with the necessary qualifications who
could help and give advice. The address of the British
Falconers' Club can always be found from the Secretary of the British Field Sports Society, 137 Victoria
Street, London, SW1.

No hawk should ever just be turned loose to take
her chance.

The code concludes with an exhortation to falconers
not to traffic in hawks, the underlying danger being
that hawks suitable for falconry might well come into
the ownership of dealers or other people with no
interest in falconry, to the possible detriment of the
hawk. It would obviously be wrong to take a hawk,
capable of being trained and flown at quarry, out of
circulation.

But there is never any difficulty about finding a
falconer who will take an unwanted hawk.

Obviously one would hope that no one aspiring to
become a falconer, or just wishing to train and fly
hawks, would need a Code of Conduct. But all
should at least read it, and know its contents, even if
only to be able to urge other folk to conform to it.

Hawk thieving

As has been mentioned already, it is no longer
exceptional to hear of trained hawks being stolen.
There is a ready market in many parts of the world for
hawks of all sorts, and a trained longwing will com-
mand a high price, perhaps £200.

One club mews in America employs a 24-hour
guard, with a dog patrolling at night, showing that
Britain is not the only country to suffer in this way.

The thieves can be divided into two distinct
categories: the professional and the amateur. The
professional may well be highly skilled in the ways of
a hawk. In the spring of 1972, one thief was known to
steal the trained hawks of no less than two falconers by
hanging about without detection near a place where
the falconers habitually flew their hawks at game or
rooks. As soon as the hawk was put on the wing and
began sweeping round in widening, mounting circles,
being a longwing, the hidden thief produced a lure of

his own, unseen by the falconer, brought the hawk to
it, 'made in' to it in rapid and professional manner,
hooded her at once and was away in his car before the
falconer had time to realize his hawk had vanished.

Since it is at the moment no offence to possess a
protected bird, only to take one, and there can usually
be no proof of the taking, the thief escapes with
impunity, and the ready market operates to his
advantage.

The other category, the amateur thief, must be
more numerous. At least one hopes so. He is at worst a
petty thief, stealing a hawk because he cannot resist
taking it, perhaps to train himself if he can get away
with it. The result is equally distressing for the falconer,
whoever steals his hawk. The hawk will probably
suffer less at the hands of the professional than of the
clandestine amateur.

Another development has been the using of trained
hawks, usually goshawks, for poaching pheasants and
other game, in conjuction with the traditional
retrieving lurcher.

143

Above left: the passage tundra falcon, chiefly used in North America, is also called the eastern or white-faced peregrine. Although very similar to the ordinary peregrine falcon, it has slightly different colouring round the head and, according to Mr. Lorant de Bastyai, shorter feet.

Above: this good-going Cooper's tiercel is belled on the breast, a method of the all-important belling which the beginner is not advised to try. It is better to start with everything in strict orthodox fashion before developing ideas of your own which may, of course, turn out better than the traditional ones.

Left: the last laugh.

Importing birds of prey

Before bringing a hawk into this country, it is necessay to have applied for a licence to do so from either the Ministry of Agriculture, Fisheries and Food, Whitehall Place, London, SW1 for England and Wales, or to the Scottish Home and Health Department, 44 York Place, Edinburgh for Scotland.

The form contains the following questions. If they are not answered fully and accurately, there may be so much delay that the bird arrives before the licence. This may lead to a lot of trouble and extra expense. The port of entry, probably an airport, since it is advisable only to use air freight, will hold a bird for a short time if they have the facilities for doing this until the licence is produced to enable the Customs to hand over the bird to her new owner.

If there is a long delay, the airport authorities will have to find a temporary home for the bird, which might be the RSPCA hostel or some other establishment. In the last resort, they may have to destroy the bird, which they are entitled to do if the delay looks like being protracted.

Application for licence to import Bird of Prey or Owl under the provision of the Protection of Birds Acts 1954 and 1967.

NOTES FOR COMPLETION

Specific answers should be given to the questions. It is particularly important that the correct names of the species to be imported should be ascertained and stated.

This form must be completed by the person who will be the owner of the bird, not by the importing Agent, if any.

Warning: Applicants are requested to give as much notice as possible of their desire to import, and should not authorize shipment before obtaining a licence. Birds imported without a licence are liable to forfeiture.

Any person who contravenes or fails to comply with the terms of an import licence is liable to prosecution.

1. Name of applicant, full address, telephone number.
2. State:
  (a) Common name of birds to be imported
  (b) Full scientific name
  (c) The number required
  (d) The sex
  (e) Whether immature or adult birds
  (f) Country of origin
3. For what purpose are the birds required?
  (a) Falconry
  (b) Educational
  (c) Agriculture
  (d) Scientific study
4. If you are applying for a licence for purposes other than falconry, state full details of your purposes, the address at which the birds will be kept (if different from that given at (c) overleaf), how the bird is to be housed (including size of aviary or other accommodation) and the numbers and species of any other birds that will occupy the same accommodation.
5. Proposed date of importation and, if known, port of entry into Great Britain.
(It is best to put one or two alternatives here, such as 'Probably London or Prestwick,' or whatever seems likely from the point of departure of the bird abroad.)
6. Name and address of overseas consignor.
7. Name and address of any dealer, agent or other person authorized to act on your behalf.
8. Personal details of applicant:
  (a) Age if under 18
  (b) Names of relevant societies of which you are a member (ornithological, agricultural or falconry)
  (c) Give details of your experience and qualifications in the field for which the birds are being imported. In the case of a licence to import a bird of prey for falconry, if you are inexperienced, state the name and address of an experienced falconer who will assist you in training the bird

If you have trained a kestrel satisfactorily before trying to import a bird, then you are not inexperienced and the latter part of this question will not apply. If this is to be your first venture, you would be better not to try to import a bird at this stage until you have built up the experience with a kestrel obtained at home.

If you do not know any experienced falconer who might help you, you would be better to wait until you

Mr. Peter Combe's tiercel peregrine, Mark, in Ross-shire, Scotland, looks distinctly bleary-eyed when offered a sip of wine.

have managed to make some contacts in the falconry world by getting in touch with one of the hawking clubs or organizations mentioned in this book.

The form concludes with a declaration, which has to be signed.

Declaration: I am the applicant for this licence. I am/am not resident in Great Britain. I declare that to the best of my knowledge and belief all the particulars in this application are correctly stated, and I undertake that if a licence is granted in response to this application, it will be used solely for the import of the birds designated herein.
Date............... Signed...........................

It is very important to make sure that your application is sent in well before there is any suggestion of your bird being despatched to you, and also that the scientific description of the proposed import is correct.

Most Customs or airport officials will not be able to tell the difference between a sakret and a lanneret (can every falconer?), which makes it all the more important to be accurate. If you are detected in any inaccuracy by a knowledgeable inspector, not only do you bring every other falconer into disrepute, but you will be liable to be blacklisted for the future by the granting Sub-Committee. There is also the possibility of prosecution, on top of all of which you may have the bird itself confiscated.

It is simpler to fill the form in correctly at the outset.

Breeding hawks in captivity

It always used to be thought that it was so difficult to breed birds of prey in captivity that it was not worth all the effort.

But during the past 10 years or so great progress in this interesting work has been made, particularly in Britain, Ireland and especially in America, where successful results have been obtained over a long period. Other enthusiasts in Czechoslovakia, Germany and other countries have followed suit. Today it is a real possibility that hawks of various sorts will breed regularly in captivity.

It is difficult to see why they should not breed

Herr Brehm's home bred goshawk receives her
morning feed by her mother in the comfort of the
nest — in this case, a lorry tyre on a table,
decorated with pine branches and twigs.

Mr. John Morris's hybrid tiercel, below and left, was the first successful achievement of a hybrid mating in 1971 between Mr. Morris's saker falcon and Mr. Ronald Stevens's peregrine tiercel, both shown in the picture on page 135.

naturally enough if the right surroundings and food are provided. There has, of course, never been any great incentive to try this as long as there was an ample supply of hawks.

But now that hawks, together with the rest of the world's wild life, are under such heavy assault from man's activities, and are losing their battle for survival, it becomes relevant to see what can be done.

One of the most notable achievements is that of the combined effort of Mr. Ronald Stevens and Mr. John Morris in Ireland. Using a saker falcon belonging to the latter, and a peregrine tiercel belonging to Mr. Stevens, a mating was achieved in an elaborately constructed form of aviary. In the first year of this effort, three eyasses were hatched, itself a remarkable achievement. One of these survived healthily. The next year three more were hatched by the same pair and on the latest reports, the whole family was doing well, see photograph, page 134.

Other people and various organizations are now taking up the work, the principle focal point in Britain being the Hawk Trust established at The Falconry Centre, near Gloucester. Under the chairmanship of Mr. Phillip Glasier, the Trust has been at work for some time on the many aspects, both practical and theoretical, of maintaining or re-establishing hawks in the wild. Research has also been undertaken by the Trust in artificial insemination of hawks, which has made progress also in America. There seems to be real hope in all these experiments of at least making a useful contribution to the survival of many species of hawks.

The way this could affect the sport of falconry is obvious enough. If enough hawks could be bred in captivity, it would not be necessary to take any birds from wild stocks at all. It is not yet clear whether a captive bred hawk would be as good from a falconry point of view as a wild bred one. But even if it were not as good in some respects, it would still be preferable to having no hawk at all.

Opinion is divided on the subject of breeding in captivity. Some see it as a way of salvation for the hawks through the supply of birds to falconers to the

149

survival of practical falconry in all its aspects. Falconry is threatened not only by the possibility of legal banning already referred to, through lack of enough people to speak up for it, but by the supply of suitable hawks drying up. Spokesmen through the various clubs and individuals in other less publicised ways are trying to fend off the former possibility. It is possible that organizations such as the Hawk Centre, reinforced by the freelance efforts of Mr. Stevens and people like him in other parts of the world, will avoid the latter.

A well-known falconer of long experience typifies the opposite school of thought in a letter to me which I quote:

'I'm afraid I think attempts at breeding birds of prey a waste of time, energy and money. Even if you do produce an aviary-bred bird, of what use is it? Can it fly and feed itself in the wild? Is it of any use to a falconer? I consider our efforts would be more usefully deployed in working for conservation in the field, such as releasing pairs of goshawks in suitable woods. The Forestry Commission could be useful allies.

'As far as peregrines, merlins and sparrowhawks are concerned, all our energies should be concentrated on (a) protection of eyries and maintenance of the law (shooting and trapping) and (b) abolition of noxious chemicals which enter the food chain.'

Most people would agree with him over the question of chemicals, with which this country is becoming saturated. But the majority might feel that breeding hawks should at least be given a good chance before judgement is pronounced.

The programmes have not been running long enough at the time of writing to show whether a useful contribution can be made or not. But the outlook seems very hopeful. The eyasses in Mr. John Morris's photograph on page 134 look normal enough in all respects. How they will perform when trained remains to be seen. American birds raised in similar conditions are reported to have flown satisfactorily for some years past.

There seems no reason why they should not be good enough for most falconry purposes.

Hawking abroad

USA AND CANADA

No modern work on hawking, however slight, would be complete without a reference to hawking in the United States.

With an uninhibited enthusiasm, North America, during the past few decades, has produced much of the finest falconry and the greatest exponents of the art which the world has probably ever seen.

They have made great strides in the breeding of captive hawks of various sorts, particularly prairie falcons, a native longwing very much like a saker or lanner, but rather browner. The eggs have been hatched mostly in incubators and there seems no trouble in bringing the young birds to maturity. There appear to be no characteristics in behaviour or flight which mark down the incubated bird from her wild sisters. There are several hawking associations in America, the chief among which is the North American Falconers' Association. Publication of the Association's annual Journal and of *Hawk Chalk* achieves world-wide circulation.

FRANCE

L'Association Nationale des Fauconniers et Autoursiers Français is particularly active, with many very distinguished French falconers and a large following of members in all stages of expertise.

The bulletin which the Association produces, called *Chasse au vol*, is particularly sought after, devoting itself to detailed records of members' activities and a great deal of thoroughly practical information, with superb illustrations.

GERMANY

Hawking is also in good and progressive hands under the Deutscherfalkenorden, the founder of which is still with them, Herr Renz Waller whom we have mentioned already. Dr. Heinz Brüll, of the Association, is the author of *Die Beizjagd* (Paul Parey, Hamburg and Berlin 1962), essential reading for anyone speaking enough German.

A meet in West Germany.

Some members of the Italian Falconers' Club, the Circolo dei Falconieri d'Italia, at a meet at Settevene. In the back row from left to right are Signor Mazza, Herr Renz Waller, Dr. Ernesto Coppaloni and Count Fulco Tosti. In the front row from left to right are Dr. del Mastro, Signor Pratesi and Dott. Caproni di Taliedo.

AUSTRIA

The *Österreichischer Falknerbund* has a hard core of very enthusiastic members who hold regular and very successful meets.

HOLLAND

The Dutch Society, the Nederland Valkenier Vebod Adriaan Mollen, thrives under more difficult conditions than some other national societies. But it is an important organization in the country where so much hawking was done in years gone by, and from which falconers, in Britain in particular, used to obtain their regular supplies of passage and haggard hawks. This supply has now come to an end unfortunately, as the famous Valkenswaard no longer has the elaborate arrangement of traps for bringing down the falcons on passage to be sent to partridge, grouse, rook and other hawking in Britain. But the sport is kept alive, thanks to the enthusiasm of the Society.

ITALY

The Circolo dei Falconieri d'Italia is a small company of falconers representing the sport in a country where all forms of wild life are particularly hard pressed through the laxity of preservational laws. The distinguished member of the Circolo, Dott. Umberto Caproni di Taliedo, is a well-known and welcome figure each year on the Caithness moors with his cadge of peregrines, and an increasing number of his compatriots are taking hawks to fly in Scotland.

SPAIN

The Centro de Cetreria is the focal point of interest in this country: Dr. F. Rodriguez de la Fuente is the well-known principal figure with many hawking friends abroad. His monumental book, *El Arte de Cetreria*, is referred to in the bibliography.

INDIA

In India very little hawking is carried out, which is sad considering the great amount that has been done there for centuries. Changed conditions have made things very difficult, but it seems possible that there may soon be a revival. At the moment, it is not easy to get any reports of what is going on in the hawking world of India. Undoubtedly a few hawks are still flown, but there would not yet seem to be any organizing society in being. It is much to be hoped that this will be rectified before too long.

Members of the Austrian Falconry Association meet
in the grounds of their Falkenhof. The
Association holds regular meets and is supported
by an increasing and enthusiastic membership.

General Sir Umar Hayat Khan, Tiwana, was one of
the best-known falconers of pre-war India and is
seen here together with another equally well-known
European falconer, Captain Charles Knight. The
Tiwana's son, Sir Khizar Hayat Khan, Tiwana, is
closely in touch with the very changed conditions
in India and Pakistan today, while Captain Knight's
nephew is Mr. Phillip Glasier, one of Europe's
foremost falconers and founder of The Falconry
Centre in Gloucestershire.

Ivan Marosi, a well-known Russian falconer, is pictured here with his eagle.

PAKISTAN

Hawking is beginning to look up after a long period in the doldrums. Several individuals are taking an increasing interest, and visitors from Germany, the Arabian States and other parts have been going to Pakistan recently. This has greatly stimulated interest in a country which is only slowly recovering from recent turmoil. When things settle down more, as in India, it is to be hoped that there will be a national revival of the long-established traditions of falconry in the country.

IRELAND

There is a long tradition of hawking in Ireland, where magpies in particular have given great sport over the years. There are several falconers of great distinction in the Irish Falconry Association, in particular Mr. Ronald Stevens and Mr. John Morris, whose breeding programme we have already noted. At Clonmel in Co. Tipperary, Herr Jocher has established a Falconry of Ireland, where he trains a variety of hawks.

JAPAN

A revival seems on the way with the establishment of a mews in the State Gardens at Nagoya, and of an official falconer to train and, presumably, to fly the several peregrines and others there already. This is a most encouraging advance from a decade ago, when the only news from Japan was of one aged falconer flying hares with a hawk eagle. He was reliably reported to be Japan's last falconer and on the verge of retirement from the sport.

The news from the State Gardens is therefore most welcome, and we look to the setting up of a national association as a result of this example. The subject has been definitively covered by the American falconer, Dr. E. W. Jameson, in conjunction with his Japanese wife, in their superb volume, *The Hawking of Japan*.

BELGIUM

There are several keen falconers in Belgium, but no national society as yet, although a committee of the Club Marie de Bourgogne has organized several meets. There is a lot of good hawking country in Belgium, so perhaps an association will soon appear.

PORTUGAL

Some hawking is now starting in this country where it used to be very popular.

MISCELLANEOUS

In several other countries, notably Switzerland, Sweden, Rhodesia, South Africa, Australia and New Zealand, and possibly others, there are many people interested in the sport and carrying it on with native birds. From reports received from individual members of these countries from time to time, the standard of sport is very high, with new people constantly coming forward to take an interest.

In Rhodesia in particular there is quite a lot of falconry practised. Peregrines, lanners, black sparrowhawks and two other smaller species are the most popular. The Rhodesian government has recently taken steps to control the export of birds of prey, and the situation is now much improved.

EPILOGUE

If the beginners' enthusiasm for the subject of hawking has carried him through to this point, then there is a good chance that falconry has gained one more supporter. It is up to him now to put the first steps into practice.

It will be difficult to start. But it is by no means impossibly difficult, and if he is really determined, he will soon experience the unique thrill of casting a hawk from his fist at some natural quarry in the full expectation of not only taking the quarry, perhaps for the larder, but also of getting his hawk back quickly and without fuss after every flight.

It is not undue discouragement to predict that he will lose his hawk at some stage through illness, accident or disaster. This has probably happened to everyone who has kept a hawk during the last 4,000 years. If one could look back along history, there would be sure to appear sooner or later, on the plains of Asia, in the sands of Egypt and Arabia, in the marshes of Wessex, a running figure whistling, panting, waving a bunch of feathers or an old rabbit skin, as he tries to recapture his lost hawk.

The beginner need have no fear of being ashamed to join in this company. This book is designed to discourage a casual approach in a sphere where the raw materials are in restricted supply. But they are not unavailable.

A genuine interest needs every encouragement and support, as does falconry itself all over the world. As has been mentioned before, this ancient sport is under heavy pressure from many sources. The fewer participants and spokesmen there are, the more easily it will be eliminated by eventual legal restrictions. There are enough hawks to go round, but they are not the same species as have been used by tradition over the centuries.

The beginner must learn all he can by reading all the books he can find, get to know other enthusiasts by joining a club, and start practical work as soon as he has done all his homework.

It is more important than ever not to waste any hawk by ignorance. I hope this book may go some little way towards stimulating a lasting interest in the subject and gaining at least a few determined and skilled supporters for this most exciting – and exacting – of all man's partnerships with the wild.

APPENDIX

Here are some addresses. These of course will change, some will disappear, new ones will take their place.

Where to buy equipment

At the time of going to press, all the hawk 'furniture' or equipment needed for any aspect of the sport, except a hawk itself, can be bought from one or more of the following:

Europe

R. C. Upton, The Leather Shop, 78 High Street, Marlborough, Wilts.

M. J. Dawson, 99 Eldred Avenue, Brighton, Sussex. Agent for Dutch made equipment, the hoods being made from the original blocks of the famous Dutch falconer, Adriaan Mollen.

A. Gates, Ken-Dor, Oak Walk, St. Peter, Jersey, for Aylmer jesses.

East

Ch. Mohammed Din & Co., Prem Gali No. 4, Railway Road, Lahore, Pakistan.

USA

Pete Asborno, 4530 W. 31st Avenue, Denver, Colorado, 80212. Bells.

H. Eugene Johnson, 2344 Nomad Avenue, Dayton, Ohio, 45414. Hoods.

Kalen Glove Manufactury, 2557 N. Dubonnet Avenue, Rosemead, California 91770. Gloves and other equipment.

Canada

Lloyd Cook, 1024 McGregor Avenue, Victoria, British Columbia, Canada. Lure with flapping wings.

The Falconry Centre

Referred to earlier in this book, the Centre is best described in the words of its founder and conductor, Mr. Phillip Glasier: 'The Falconry Centre has been established not only as a rendezvous for hawking enthusiasts, whether old hands, or students of this ancient sport, but also for anyone interested in a country pursuit which has for centuries formed a part of the traditional pattern of our national heritage. The aim of the Centre is to be a clearing house for the exchange of information, experience, advice and news between falconers everywhere, as well as being an interesting place to visit.

'There is a museum showing the different birds used in falconry, their equipment and how it is made, methods of training and ways of trapping, and much else besides.

'There is a Hawk Walk, which is a collection of trained birds, British and Foreign, from golden eagles to falconets, each properly jessed and leashed. There is an aviary of less distinguished birds of prey such as owls, kites and caracaras, a flying ground where falcons are shown in training and being flown to the lure.

'There are lectures, films and demonstrations, and also courses are run, not only for absolute beginners, but also for those whose relations with their birds may not be as happy as they might wish.'

Address: The Falconry Centre, Newent, Glos.

BIBLIOGRAPHY

It is a great encouragement for the future of the whole realm of falconry that during the last two decades or so, many new books on falconry have been published. An additional most helpful development has been the reprinting by modern processes of many of the old time classics which had been put far beyond the reach of the majority of beginners by their scarcity value.

Conditions today, however, are unrecognizably different from when most of the standard works were written. They contain abundant information on the keeping and flying of all sorts of hawk but much of it, although of great interest, is, naturally, very out of date and quite inapplicable to the modern hawker or falconer.

The beginner should not wade through too much material until he has had enough experience to distinguish the wood from the trees and to recognize what is applicable to his circumstances. After this, he may well want to get hold of anything that has ever been published. If so, his pocket will need to be very deep indeed.

But until that stage is reached, the following modern books will make a very good basis for a library. A fuller bibliography appears in *Falconry For You*, noted below.

Falconry For You by Humphrey ap Evans (Foyle's). A comprehensive 'next stage' for beginners who have absorbed *Introduction To Falconry*.
As The Falcon Her Bells by Phillip Glasier. Autobiography of the well known falconer.
Hunting Bird From A Wild Bird by Lorent de Bastyai. A delightful book by the colourful Hungarian falconer.
A Falcon In The Field and *A Hawk For The Bush* by J. Mavrogordato, two modern classics by the former President of the British Falconers' Club.
The Goshawk by T. H. White. Instructive, humorous saga.
A Manual Of Falconry by Michael Woodford. A full treatise by the former Secretary of the British Falconers' Club.
Falcons And Falconry by Frank Illingworth. Cheerfully discoursive and informative.

It is worth writing for their lists to the following publishers who have been reprinting some of the old books at reasonable prices:
1. Standfast Press, Frampton-on-Severne, Glos.
2. Thames Valley Press, Maidenhead, Berks.
3. Tideline Books, Clun, Salop.
4. Bernard Quaritch, Golden Square, London W1.
5. The Holland Press, 112 Whitfield St., London W1.
6. The Coptic Press, 7 Coptic Street, London WC1.
7. The Falcon Head Press, P.O. Box 913, Golden, Colorado, 80401, USA.

From abroad

America
North American Falconry And Hunting Hawks. A distillation of the most advanced practice and theory in modern American falconry. Superlative illustrations. Very well worth obtaining.

Japan
The Hawking of Japan by Dr. E. W. Jameson and his Japanese wife. Of great interest, with much detail on Japanese methods.

France
Traité de Fauconnerie et Autourserie. Although published in 1948, this is the French handbook which has not, I think, yet been superseded.

Germany
Der Wilde Falk ist mein Gesell by Renz Waller 1962. The first volume by the doyen of German falconry. Very comprehensive, as would be expected from such an authority.
Die Beizjagd by Dr. Heinz Brüll, a work of great interest and distinction from the President of the Deutscherfalken-orden.

Italy
Falconeria Moderna by Francesco Pestellini. There does not seem to have been anything more recent than this very fully illustrated treatise published in 1941. It is doubtful whether there would be much to add to it.

Spain
El Arte de Cetreria by Felix Rodriguez de la Fuente. A truly superlative work, brilliantly illustrated and vastly comprehensive. There can surely be nothing about modern falconry left unsaid. Well worth having even if you speak no Spanish.